The
EVERYTHING®
Sign Language Book

Dear Reader:

As the parent of a son who was born profoundly deaf, I quickly realized how important it was for my son to communicate with those who were involved in his daily world. I also realized—after exploring a number of other methods—that signing was the most effective way for him to communicate. Sign language allowed him to express his needs and to share what was on his mind with other people.

It wasn't so long ago that books, instructional guides, and education in sign language were generally designed for those who were deaf and hard of hearing. Books were often difficult to understand or imitate, and they left many questions unanswered. *The Everything® Sign Language Book* is "user-friendly," and it is my hope that you will find this book to be an easy and pleasant journey into the wonderful world of sign language.

Over the past twenty years, I have taught courses, workshops, and in-services to those who have desired to learn American Sign Language. I have seen how hard work and enthusiasm for learning can open the door to sign language and lead to improved communication for all. My wish for you is to learn from this book, enjoy what you learn, and, most importantly, use what you learn.

Sincerely,

The EVERYTHING® Series

Editorial

Publishing Director	Gary M. Krebs
Managing Editor	Kate McBride
Copy Chief	Laura MacLaughlin
Acquisitions Editor	Eric M. Hall
Development Editor	Lesley Bolton
Production Editor	Khrysti Nazzaro
	Jaime Wielgus
Technical Reviewer	Douglas Dunn

Production

Production Director	Susan Beale
Production Manager	Michelle Roy Kelly
Series Designers	Daria Perreault
	Colleen Cunningham
Cover Design	Paul Beatrice
	Frank Rivera
Layout and Graphics	Colleen Cunningham
	Rachael Eiben
	Michelle Roy Kelly
	Daria Perreault
	Erin Ring
Series Cover Artist	Barry Littmann

Visit the entire Everything® Series at everything.com

THE
EVERYTHING
SIGN
LANGUAGE
BOOK

American Sign Language
made easy

Irene Duke

Adams Media
Avon, Massachusetts

This book is for David; for my past, present, and future students; and for so many other people who could benefit from a better understanding of sign language!

An Everything® Series Book.
Everything® and everything.com® are registered trademarks of F+W Publications, Inc.

Published by Adams Media, an F+W Publications Company
57 Littlefield Street, Avon, MA 02322 U.S.A.
www.adamsmedia.com

ISBN: 1-58062-882-6
Printed in the United States of America.

J I H G F E D

Library of Congress Cataloging-in-Publication Data
Duke, Irene.
The everything sign language book / Irene Duke.
p.   cm.
(An everything series book)
ISBN 1-58062-882-6
1. American Sign Language. I. Title. II. Series: Everything series.

HV2474.D85 2004
419'.7–dc21

2003014708

This book is available at quantity discounts for bulk purchases.
For information, call 1-800-872-5627.

Contents

10

11

12

13

Acknowledgments

I wish to express my appreciation to the wonderful staff of the Whitman-Hanson Regional School District for their encouragement and support, who took the time each week to inquire, "How is the book coming?" A special thank-you goes to W-H technology for their assistance in helping me to resolve my untimely computer problems. I send forth sincere gratitude to my mentor, Beth, for the many years she has provided me with guidelines to writing and for her lasting friendship. In addition, my sincerest thanks to my kind friend and coworker, Genie, who provided me with daily support and the faith that this book would become a reality. My gratitude is also extended to all of my students from Massasoit College, to the Early Childcare providers, and to the participants of the many American Sign Language (ASL) in-services and workshops, who provided me with endless resources and constant inspiration. A warm thanks to Lesley Bolton for her work in smoothing out all the edges in the manuscript and a huge thank-you to Eric Hall for his encouragement and support. My greatest appreciation is given to my friend and sister, who burnt the midnight oil with me, held my hand, and spent hours every weekend typing. I do not know how I could have managed to bring this book to fruition without all her efforts. Finally, I am sending my loving appreciation to my husband for his endless support and his constant unconditional love.

Top Ten Reasons
You Should Learn Sign Language

1. To be able to communicate effectively with the Deaf and hard of hearing.
2. To improve your nonverbal communication skills.
3. To broaden language acquisition in children.
4. It looks great on a resume and can open doors of new employment opportunities.
5. To learn a new language.
6. It opens new avenues for friendships and relationships.
7. It will help you broaden your horizons and provide you with an alternate way of expressing yourself.
8. It spurs intellectual growth.
9. To improve your public speaking skills and self-confidence.
10. It's fun!

Introduction

▶ IT'S OBVIOUS that you're interested in sign language because otherwise you wouldn't have picked up this book. But did you know that you already use a natural form of gestural sign language everyday? Nodding your head "yes," shaking your head "no," telling someone to call by holding an imaginary phone to your ear, or saying hello with a friendly wave are all natural gestures. With those natural gestures and this book in hand, you have already given yourself a wonderful head start into learning the basics of sign language.

This sign language book is user-friendly. It is designed to acclimate you slowly into the various parts of sign language while being fun at the same time. It is not meant to be a heavy textbook, or a sign language dictionary. It is concise in detail and filled with fantastic sign images that use real models. Each chapter offers an easy and cumulative learning experience, and signs are presented in a progressive pattern.

While this book can be used on its own, it can also be used in conjunction with an American Sign Language (ASL) class and, of course, natural language acquisition through interactions with deaf friends and relatives. In that case, this book would serve as a friendly bridge between the classroom, sign dictionary, and text. It will also fill in the gray areas those new signers often find confusing or challenging. You will acquire a better understanding of the various applications for sign language and the population that uses this visual mode of communication.

Perhaps you are a person who has studied different languages, but you never received any real gratification—and certainly not instant gratification—from those studies. ASL is different from these other languages in that if you follow the easy-to-read instructions, you will be able to form signs quickly. The basic signs are easy to learn, and before you know it, you will be stringing them together in short sentences. This is true even if you are a person whose life is punctuated by constant interruptions—you will be able to pick up this book and put it down at your leisure and still learn!

You can share the learning experience with family and friends by having them watch while you form the signs and see if you are signing it the way the images appear in the book. You can encourage them to learn with you and try to hold conversations using simple signs and hand gestures. A parent of young children can practice the basic signs while reading to her children, thus enhancing story time and giving the kids a head start in their own acquisition of ASL when their language acquisition skills are most keen. Even a trip to the zoo can be made more interactive for yourself and your children with the use of signs.

You will be able to teach others the letters of the alphabet and practice fingerspelling words—this, of course, is after you have learned to sign all the letters of the alphabet. Some of the basic signs that are introduced here could be just enough for you to provide a patient in a hospital, for example, some comfort and companionship until an interpreter arrives. Then again, this book may spark enough interest that you consider changing careers and seeking out that special job that requires communicating with a diverse population. Regardless of whether you have the opportunity to use sign language with a deaf or hard of hearing person, you will still be enriched by learning American Sign Language.

Chapter 1

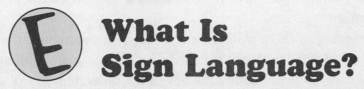

What Is Sign Language?

S ign language is a visual mode of communication and the third most-used language in the world. There is a great deal to learn about this language, its types, and its users. So let's push open the doors and enter the fascinating world of American Sign Language (ASL).

A Visual Mode of Communication

Most languages are based on audible sounds. People are naturally accustomed to language that is spoken, and for many of us, daily communication is received and understood through hearing. However, sign language is a *visually* based form of communication. It is received through our powers of vision and understood as a seen, rather than heard, language.

In the signing world, it is important to know and recognize the primary types of sign language. Therefore, before going any further, let's concentrate on learning about a few of the different types of sign language. While there are several, the next sections will focus on the five most commonly known types: American Sign Language, Signed Exact English, Pidgin Sign English/Contact Sign, Home Signs, and Fingerspelling.

American Sign Language

American Sign Language, known as ASL, is the natural native language of the American Deaf community. ASL is used as the primary mode of communication in the daily lives of the Deaf. Even so, there is a portion of the deaf population that does not use ASL. The reasons for this can range from personal choice to parental influences, educational philosophies, or regional and geographical locations.

Oftentimes, people are under the misconception that ASL is just a form of manual English. On the contrary, ASL is a separate living, natural language that has developed over the years within the Deaf community. ASL is a full language with its own grammar and structure, composed of precise handshapes and movements.

QUESTION?

Why is a capital "D" used in the word Deaf?
It is used to create a distinction. The lowercase word "deaf" refers to the physical condition of hearing loss. The uppercase word "Deaf" refers to the Deaf community, which shares a common language, cultural heritage, and similar interests.

These movements and handshapes, supported by facial expressions and body language, are capable of conveying complex and abstract ideas as well as humor, wit, and poetry. The following combined elements serve to make ASL an exciting, effective mode of communication:

- ASL signs
- Limited fingerspelling
- Facial expressions
- Body language
- Head movement
- Use of space and directional movement

Signed Exact English

Signed Exact English, known as SEE, is an English-based sign system. This system uses ASL signs that are extended with English prefixes, suffixes, endings, and tenses. Because of this composition, SEE is used in various educational settings. The focus in this type of sign application is to enhance and promote English and its grammar while building reading and writing skills. SEE can be found in legal situations or in a court of law where it is legally imperative to demonstrate every word. This form of signing has also been adopted by hearing parents who may feel more comfortable with the strong English order.

Additional signing time is required when using SEE because of the many add-on elements needed for each signed word. Also, in this system, one word is equal to one sign, and these signs are presented in exact English word order. Here are some of the elements that comprise SEE:

- Standard signs
- Fingerspelling
- Initialization (see Chapter 4)
- Prefixes
- Suffixes
- Endings
- One word equals one sign
- English word order

Pidgin Sign English/Contact Sign

Pidgin Sign English, known as PSE or Contact Sign, is a sign system that uses ASL signs in English word order. PSE/Contact Sign is often used to help bridge the communication gap between the deaf, Deaf community, and hearing. This is especially true in situations where a signer has limited ASL skills. PSE/Contact Sign allows signers to keep up with English word order by omitting prefixes, suffixes, endings, and small words.

Perhaps it is best to describe the PSE/Contact Sign system as a cross between English and ASL. Often it is used as a transitional step in the process of acclimating someone into ASL. Depending on the skills of the signer, this system can vary in degrees between English and ASL.

PSE/Contact Sign is used by a number of educators, employers, service-providers, and hearing parents of deaf children. Often, students new to the study of ASL use PSE/Contact Sign in their learning stages. In addition, a percentage of late-deafened adults adopt PSE/Contact Sign as a support method of communication. They have expressed a sense of comfort with the English order of ASL signs. This is quite natural as English is their first language.

FACT

Total Communication, referred to as TC, uses all means available for communication: sign language, gesturing, lip reading, fingerspelling, speech, hearing aids, reading, writing, and visual images.

Characteristics of PSE/Contact Sign include the following:

- Standard signs
- ASL signs
- Fingerspelling

- Facial expressions
- Body language
- English word order

Home Signs

Home Signs are invented signs that are combined with some standard ASL or SEE signs, pantomime, and natural gestures. Home Signs are invented primarily out of necessity. This type of signing occurs when sign language or a specific sign for a word is not known. This inventive approach to language is a normal progression. It often occurs with young children and in situational groups.

During the course of a week, perhaps without realizing it, we create special words for family, workplaces, and things. These affectionate names are then only recognized within our close circles of friends, coworkers, and family members. Home Signs function in much the same way. It would not be unusual, not knowing the proper signs for nouns, to see a young Deaf child signing "brown balls" to represent a cocoa-flavored cereal or "purple drink" for grape juice. So as you become more aware of the different types of sign language, be on the lookout for Home Signs that use descriptive adjectives rather than properly signed names and nouns.

Fingerspelling

Fingerspelling is a way of representing a word by spelling it out, letter by letter. It uses the American Manual Alphabet, which is a set of separate handshapes representing each of the twenty-six letters of the English alphabet. Watching and reading every letter of each word is exhausting and you will need to keep this in mind. ASL uses limited fingerspelling. However, fingerspelling and the handshapes of the manual alphabet do play important roles in signing. You will get a better understanding of this technique in Chapter 4.

What You Will Learn

Now that you have a major portion of the technical information behind you, try your hand at a pop quiz. Without looking back, can you remember what these acronyms represent?

- ASL
- SEE
- PSE

If you answered American Sign Language, Signed Exact English, and Pidgin Sign English, good for you! Applause, applause! It is important to remember these three acronyms. Once you venture into the signing world, you will find that they are used repeatedly in discussions of types of sign language. It is quite common to be asked what type of signing you know and use and where you acquired your skill. As you move forth into the rest of this book, you will see the acronym ASL used throughout, as this type of sign language will be our primary focus. The term "sign language" will be used only as a generic form.

Basic Vocabulary

You will soon acquire a basic sign vocabulary. Add just a little daily practice and a smidge of determination, and you will be well on your way to reaching the first level of signing proficiency. To make your learning journey much more interesting and easy to comprehend, this book includes hundreds of detailed images of standard signs. Please note that all of the images show what you see when another person is facing you and signing (or, in other words, what another person will see when you make this sign to communicate with them). Just take a close look at this image, which illustrates the sign for "hello.

▲ **HELLO:** The starting point of the hand position is quite similar to a military salute. Now, simply wave your hand off your forehead.

Signs and Rules

Soon, you will learn many signs pertaining to people, emotions, questions, food, time, travel, medical situations, and much more. You will learn the basic rules for fingerspelling, sign order, facial expression, and body language. In addition, you will learn strategies to make learning sign language easy and fun. You will also acquire knowledge of the particular framework that sets sign language apart from spoken languages.

FACT

Just as spoken language varies in different places throughout the world, sign language is not the same everywhere you go. Presently, there are at least 200 different forms in existence worldwide.

There are also rules regarding signing etiquette and rules regarding the American Disabilities Act that will be presented. Moreover, there are important do's and don'ts to learn regarding the deaf, the Deaf community, and the hard of hearing in medical situations. Of course, there will be many little tidbits of information to enjoy and to build on. Now, let us move on and find out about people, just like you, who are interested in sign language.

Who Uses Sign Language?

First and foremost, sign language is used by the Deaf community, the hard of hearing, the deaf/blind, and interpreters for the deaf. In addition, it is used by parents, family, friends, and service providers for the deaf and the Deaf community who support the use of signing as a way to communicate.

In general, just as with many other things in life, changes and expansions occur. This is ever so true with the evolving language of signs. The use of sign language now has expanded into many various settings that are not related to the deaf population. An example of this is demonstrated by the application of sign language in educational settings. Educational applications can range from enhancement of language in young children to its use in assisting communication within the highly diverse special-needs population. (However, it must be noted that the use of this type of basic sign language does not and cannot compare to the pure ASL used within the Deaf community.)

An interpreter is a person who facilitates communication for the Deaf, the hard of hearing, and hearing persons by translating spoken language into sign language.

Whatever your reasons are for learning and using sign language, they can only result in giving you a positive effect and experience. Perhaps you will find your occupation or special interest mentioned in the sections that follow. Or maybe your reasons are simply based on a fascination with this visual language. Let's take a look at the occupations and special interests that often require skill in sign language.

Special-Needs Educators

Special-needs educators are applying visual signs to stimulate, ease, and assist communication. Often, within the challenged population, the signs adopted for use are modified or simplified. Using modified signs accommodates the diverse challenges of special-needs children and adults alike. Each year, the rate of special-needs educators who adopt visual signs increases for use within a classroom setting. Special-needs job trainers and various service providers who are involved with independent living programs are also using signs as a means of supporting communication and providing information.

Regular Educators

Regular educators in high schools and colleges are beginning to support the acceptance of ASL as a second language. More courses in sign language are now being taught for academic credit in many world and foreign language programs.

Educators working within regular educational systems are witnessing the enrichment that ASL brings to the lives of their students. Today, you will see ASL students in upper grades of high schools go into the lower grades and share their knowledge. They stage fun-filled demonstrations in sign language to the delight of the younger students. You also can find these same students applying their signing skills in community service and after-school programs. These students often continue in secondary education, majoring in Deaf studies. They also become the greatly needed interpreters or service providers for the deaf, the Deaf community, and the hard of hearing.

FACT

In 1989, the U.S. Supreme Court recognized American Sign Language as a standard independent language with its own grammar, syntax, vocabulary, and cultural heritage. This court ruled that ASL could be offered in all public and secondary schools to satisfy foreign language requirements.

This refreshing new fascination with ASL as a second language piques an interest in teachers and paraprofessionals. School systems are now starting to offer basic ASL courses for their staff as well. The goal is to bring this language into the classroom to enhance language and communication skills. As a result, teachers and support staff are also reaping the benefits that come from the acceptance of ASL as a second language in educational systems.

Children of Deaf Adults

Today, there is a higher probability that students whose parents are Deaf will be enrolling into a public school system. These students are known as "CODAs" within the Deaf community. CODA, or Children of Deaf Adults, are bilingual and bicultural as a result of the Deaf environment in which they grow up. Yet at the same time, these children also live, socialize, and attend schools in the hearing world. The acronym KODA, or Kids of Deaf Adults, represents the younger portion of this population.

The need for sign language, in this type of situation, would have a double purpose. First, ASL would likely be the primary method of communication for members of the Deaf community who are parents.

Signing would be required for effective communication between the parents and school personnel. Deaf parents are generally pleased to learn that a school has staff members who can sign, even if their signing skills are basic. Basic signing skills can serve as a bridge until an interpreter arrives for meetings or teacher conferences. These simple signing skills can also provide helpful information in the event there is an emergency involving the child. It is important to remember that the Americans with Disabilities Act, or ADA, mandates that an interpreter be provided to ensure that Deaf parents receive equal access to communication.

FACT

The Americans with Disabilities Act is a federal civil rights law protecting individuals with disabilities. It guarantees individuals with disabilities equal opportunity and access to state and local government services, public accommodations, employment, transportation, and telecommunications.

The second application of sign language would be for the ease and comfort of the KODA student into a classroom setting. In all probability, ASL will be the student's first language. Signing, to some degree, may be necessary to support spoken language and ease the first year of school for the young bilingual student of Deaf parents.

Early Childhood Educators and Child Care Providers

Early childhood educators and child care providers are using sign language to enhance language acquisition and build cognitive skills. Through the efforts of these educators and providers, young children are able to experience the fun that comes from learning signed vocabulary. Excitement fills the air as young children learn signs through a variety of games, signed stories, and of course, singing and signing songs. At the same time, these providers are also instilling children with an awareness and sensitivity towards children who have verbal, mental, and physical challenges. They are able to teach children that signing is simply another way of communicating and that it is okay to be different.

Public Employees

Police officers, firefighters, and first responders have gained an interest in sign language. Many have completed courses in ASL or are presently enrolled. This, in turn, is improving access to communication for the deaf, the Deaf community, and the hard of hearing when the need arises for services provided by public employees. In addition, this interest has benefited all involved by promoting positive attitudes and awareness toward the deaf.

Medical Personnel

Medical professionals, such as doctors, nurses, emergency medical technicians, paramedics, and hospital staff, are quickly realizing the advantages of knowing basic sign language. In the medical community, it is becoming more common for doctors and hospitals to be visited by deaf adults.

A very large percentage of these deaf adults are part of what is known as the "Rubella Bulge" of the 1960s. Also called the German Measles Epidemic, the Rubella Bulge created an enormous surge in incidences of deafness. Of those pregnant women who contracted German measles, or rubella, an extraordinarily high number had infants who were born with birth defects. These defects ranged from deafness, heart conditions, and blindness to complicated multiple birth defects. Between 1963 and 1965 alone, over 30,000 Rubella babies were born. The estimated rate of deafness was 73 percent.

Sign language interpreters who are trained in medical signs should always be used when a deaf patient is unable to comfortably communicate or comprehend information. In addition, interpreters must be provided when medical diagnoses, treatment, and information is complex, according to the ADA.

Today, this portion of the Deaf population ranges in age from the thirties to late forties. They are now starting to experience their share of medical concerns and problems. Members of various medical communities are learning basic signs. The goal is to help ease frustrations experienced by deaf patients in communicating some of their basic medical needs.

Presently, sign language classes boast a high enrollment of medical personnel. If the medical profession is your future interest or line of work, you will be pleased to know that in this book, there is an entire chapter dedicated to the medical field. (See Chapter 16 for more information.)

Service Providers

Service providers working in the following areas are exposed daily to a large percentage of the public. The probability of encountering a deaf or hard-of-hearing person who is seeking services from any of these areas increases with every passing year:

- Federal, state, and town agencies
- Postal services, banks, transportation
- Restaurants, retailers, hotels, theaters
- Libraries, parks, museums
- Ministries, churches, synagogues

The enormous increase in the deafened population that resulted from the German Measles Epidemic has and will have far-reaching effects on service providers. Today, the population of the Rubella Bulge is thriving. Many are now adult members of contributing Deaf communities who have spread out all across the country. Many are married, have children, pay taxes, own cars, and support homes. They live their daily lives no differently than the average American. Keep in mind, this also means they are consumers of products and services in all areas. The chances of anyone's meeting, providing services to, or employing members of this Deaf community continuously increase.

Chapter 2

The Origins and History of Sign Language

Early evolution of sign language—that is, before the eighteenth century—remains unclear. However, there have been significant events and contributions to this ever-changing, living language. In this chapter, we will stroll through a few of the interesting pathways that have led to the development of sign language in America.

The Beginning

Try to imagine language in prehistoric times. It is easy to visualize a gestural sign language that members of a tribe might have used among themselves on a hunt. For instance, these hunters might have gestured to one another to maintain silence while hunting their wild game. Now move a little forward in time, and imagine how languages crossed and mixed as the world's population spread across the continents. As one language met a new, strange tongue, it is very probable that natural, gestural signing would have occurred while people figured out how to bridge their language gaps.

A Native System of Sign Language

People from the earliest of days to the present communicate to some degree using their hands. Therefore, long before the documented events of the nineteenth century, it can be surmised that a native system of sign language existed among deaf people. In all probability, this deaf population would have used regional, geographical, or indigenous sign systems. They also would have created their own signs, such as the Home Signs discussed in Chapter 1. There is an interesting American historical record describing such an example between the seventeenth and nineteenth centuries on Martha's Vineyard.

Vineyard Sign Language

An example of an indigenous sign language community existed on Martha's Vineyard, an island just off the coast of Cape Cod, Massachusetts. It was here, from the late 1600s through the early 1900s, that the hearing population and the Deaf community developed and used a native sign language system. An extraordinarily high rate of genetic deafness on the island perpetuated the use of the Vineyard Sign Language, as it is called. Due to intermarriage among the islanders, this high rate of genetic deafness continued for 200 years.

Nonetheless, this community flourished, with hearing and Deaf islanders working and signing side by side. Vineyard Sign Language was handed down from generation to generation through the native signers. With the arrival of deaf education on the mainland, the lives of the population began to change. Deaf children attended new residential schools on the mainland, bringing with them their native sign language.

FACT

According to census reports, deafness in the American population during the nineteenth century occurred in one person out of every 6,000. The rate for deafness on Martha's Vineyard, however, was one in 155.

On the mainland, these children eventually found spouses, married, and settled down to live. Thus began the gradual decline in the numbers of the Deaf islanders on Martha's Vineyard. But, at the same time, a new growth began, as Vineyard Signs added to and merged with ASL signs on the mainland.

The Creators

It was during the eighteenth century that sign language began to take a recorded shape in history. Beginning in France in the 1700s, Abbé Charles Michel de l'Epee opened the first free school that served as a shelter for the deaf. The school supplied food, housing, and, most importantly, education. Abbé de l'Epee studied and mastered the natural French signs of the deaf, called Old French Sign Language (OFSL). However, he believed these French signs were lacking in grammar.

Abbé Charles Michel de l'Epee

Abbé de l'Epee, being creative and with charitable intentions, modified the grammar of these signs. This resulted in a methodical signed version of spoken French, called Old Sign French (OSF). What l'Epee perhaps failed to realize was that, in all probability, OFSL had its own grammar, just as ASL has its own grammar. The impact of these grammar modifications by l'Epee were later realized in the history, studies, and debates of sign language in America. Today, there is a question whether OSF was an early form of Signed English, as described in Chapter 1.

Later, Abbé de l'Epee trained Abbé Roch Sicard in Old Sign French. Sicard became a teacher of the deaf and a school director. A significant contribution to sign language was made by Abbé Sicard in 1782, with his writing of an elaborate dictionary of signs, *Theory of Signs.*

Thomas Gallaudet

Thomas Gallaudet, an American Congregational minister, met Abbé Sicard in 1816 while in search of methods to educate deaf children. He also met a deaf man by the name of Laurent Clerc. Clerc was Sicard's protégé and chief assistant and was considered a master teacher. So impressed was Gallaudet with Clerc—who was fluent in OSF, OFSL, and French—that he invited him to America to establish the first school for the deaf.

In 1816, Clerc and Gallaudet set sail on a fifty-five-day voyage to America. During this time, Clerc taught Gallaudet Old Sign French, and Gallaudet tutored Clerc in English. On April 15, 1817, they opened the first school for the deaf. The school was in Connecticut, with seven students enrolled. Gallaudet served as principal and Clerc the head teacher.

The first established school for the deaf was called the Connecticut Asylum at Hartford for the Instruction of Deaf and Dumb Persons. Today, this school is known as The American School for the Deaf, with more than 4,000 alumni over its long history.

Gallaudet advocated and lectured for the education of the deaf. He married deaf alumna Sophia Fowler and started a large family of CODAs. Gallaudet retired from the Hartford school in 1830 and devoted his time to his ministries and writings supporting deaf education and sign language.

He also devoted time to writing children's books. He died in 1851, at the age of sixty-four, leaving behind a remarkable legacy in deaf education.

Laurent Clerc

Laurent Clerc taught and advocated for the deaf in America for forty-one years. During that time, he trained future hearing and deaf teachers. These future teachers spread out across America, teaching and establishing schools using Clerc's teaching methods.

In 1818, Laurent Clerc successfully went before the U.S. Congress to gain support for deaf education. He was the first deaf person to address Congress. Thirty residential schools were established during Clerc's lifetime, a credit to his great influence in deaf education of that period. Clerc's Old Sign French blended with the modified and indigenous signs of the students. Today, it is believed that this melding eventually evolved into what is now known as American Sign Language.

The Golden Age of Deaf Education

Between the years 1818 and 1912, more than thirty schools for the deaf were established. These schools were established by deaf teachers, hearing teachers, and deaf students who were alumni of the American School for the Deaf and Gallaudet College.

Gallaudet College was established in Washington, D.C., in 1864. It was and still remains the only liberal arts college exclusively for the deaf, both in the United States and in the world. Originally, the college was named the Columbia Institution for the Instruction of the Deaf and Dumb and the Blind. By the request of the alumni, in 1893, the name of the college was changed to honor Thomas Hopkins Gallaudet.

Gallaudet's son, Edward Miner Gallaudet, became the first president of Gallaudet College. Speaking of presidents, here are some little-known involvements between the college and United States presidents. Abraham Lincoln signed an act of Congress establishing accreditation for Gallaudet College and was its first patron. Ronald Reagan accorded university status to Gallaudet College in 1986. And in a tradition that began with Ulysses S.

Grant in 1869, the president of the United States, as patron of the university, signs all diplomas.

Between years 1840 and 1912, American Sign Language flourished across the United States. These years were known as the Golden Age of Deaf Education, and approximately 40 percent of all the deaf educators were deaf themselves. Sadly, this golden age went into a downslide near the end of the nineteenth century.

The Dark Age of Sign Language History

In 1880, the Milan Congress on Education for the Deaf voted to abolish the use of sign language in deaf education. Instead, oralism was adopted as the preferred method in deaf education worldwide. Oralism was a technique used in educating the deaf that relied solely on lip-reading, speech, and auditory training, instead of using signs. As the oralism method in deaf education began to take hold, it brought about what can be called the Dark Age of Deaf history.

FACT

The oralist approach became deeply rooted in the state of Massachusetts. In 1867, the Clarke School in Northampton was established, becoming the first truly oral school for the deaf.

Institutions that used sign language were reformed, and hundreds of oral schools were opened. Some states adopted laws prohibiting the use of signing in public schools. Deaf students were punished and reprimanded. Deaf teachers across the country lost their positions during this transition into oralism. However, children in oral schools clandestinely signed in dorms and play areas. It was with tenacity that ASL survived the suppression.

Manualism versus Oralism

The great debate between proponents of manualism (signing) and supporters of oralism raged on, and after 200 years, some differences still separate the parties. This was evidenced in 1995 when Miss Alabama, Heather Whitestone, who is deaf, won the coveted title of Miss America.

Whitestone was criticized for choosing to speak rather than use sign language. Again, the debate was sparked, and it received front-page attention within the Deaf community.

Is Sign Language Really a "Language"?

Another debate raged over the question of whether sign language was a true language or a string of simple gestures. Dr. William C. Stokoe Jr., known as the father of ASL, proved in 1960 that American Sign Language meets all the requisite linguistic criteria to be classified as a fully developed language. His research work and the books he published brought about the acceptance of ASL as an appropriate language of instruction for the deaf, in addition to its status as an appropriate second language for hearing students in higher education. Dr. Stokoe was a tireless advocate for the linguistic and educational rights of the Deaf, and he continued to actively write and publish until his death in 2000.

A Year Worth Remembering

In 1988, a new and respected heroine made her entrance into the chapters of sign language and Deaf history. Deaf actress Marlee Matlin captured the Oscar for Best Actress in her role in *Children of a Lesser God*. Matlin, who uses sign language, has continued to work in many acting roles, such as those she had played in the television series *The West Wing*, *Picket Fences*, and *Reasonable Doubts*. To date, Marlee has appeared in all kinds of roles in more than thirty movies and television programs. Much is owed to Marlee Matlin, who with her fame brought about awareness and exposure to the use of sign language.

It is important to remember that one cannot separate sign language history from the history of the Deaf community. Pure ASL belongs to the Deaf community with its rich and tenacious history. Throughout the remaining chapters, you will find informational pieces on the deaf, the Deaf community, and its culture. In addition, you will find resources for further studies on this subject in Appendix B.

At the same time, in 1988, an extraordinary and significant event took place in the annals of Deaf history. Students at Gallaudet University in Washington, D.C., staged a weeklong protest and brought national attention to their revolutionary demand for a "Deaf President Now." Gallaudet students forced the closure of the campus with their demand for the appointment of a Deaf president. The revolt was sparked when Elizabeth Ann Zinser, the only hearing candidate of a field of three finalists, was voted president. Zinser had relatively little experience with ASL or the Deaf population. Support grew throughout the week for the issue and the protesting students' agenda. These were their four demands:

1. Appointment of a Deaf president.
2. Resignation of chairwoman Jane Spillman, who spoke unfavorably of the Deaf.
3. The board of trustees would be comprised of Deaf members, representing 51 percent.
4. No repercussions for those involved in the protest.

On Friday, March 11, 1988, 3,000 protesters marched to the U.S. Capitol building with their demands. By Sunday, all their demands had been met, and Dr. I. King Jordan was appointed the first Deaf president of Gallaudet University. This victory was an exceptional turning point for members of the Deaf community, their culture, identity, and their beloved language.

Sign Language Today

The influences of Old Sign French can still be seen in American Sign Language today. Further linguistic studies are taking place, and the work of Stokoe, the father of ASL, endures. Marlee Matlin and her work as an actress continues, while at the same time she serves as a role model to many. Heather Whitestone, Miss America of 1995, is still capturing media attention with her recent cochlear implant. Gallaudet is a bustling campus with approximately 1,850 students. It continues to grow and offers a vast array of programs and research centers. The university boasts 14,000 alumni, nationally and internationally.

Today, ASL is alive and thriving and has its place in deaf education. Parents of deaf children have multiple choices in education. The Deaf community and its culture are holding fast with their consistent tenacity. The deaf population who were part of the 1960s rubella epidemic population are active and contributing to the everyday economy. All of this brings us right back to the points discussed in Chapter 1, namely, the need in society today for people who are familiar with sign language. You, the reader, are one of those people.

History has shown there will always be a need for the use of sign language. ASL will, therefore, remain a thriving, constantly evolving language. In addition, it will always be a language that enriches the lives of all those who become involved with its use.

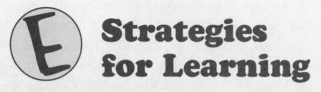

Chapter 3

Strategies for Learning

You're going to learn sign language slowly and steadily, moving one chapter at a time. Each chapter acts as a building block. In this chapter, you will learn which is your dominant signing hand, gain valuable learning strategies, and get to know some rules and elements of ASL. Push up your sleeves, and get ready to work!

Early ASL Awkwardness

Don't be afraid of making errors. Remember: To err is human. Everyone makes mistakes. It's really no big deal if you make an error while learning ASL. It's all just part of the learning process and has no serious consequences. Your mistakes might even produce a few laughs! Silly signing errors happen consistently in beginning-level ASL classes. Just have a good giggle, move on, and learn from your errors.

Whatever you do, don't get discouraged. Don't give up, and never say "can't." You *can* learn ASL, and you *will* have fun doing it. Although there are no shortcuts to learning how to form each sign, there is plenty of support in these pages. With a little determination, a positive attitude, and a dab of courage, you'll be signing with confidence in no time.

Those new to ASL often express frustration and discomfort during the first few weeks of learning. Have patience until you get past the awkward stage. You may experience these feelings:

- You are not in control of your arms and hands.
- You have no idea why your hands formed a particular sign.
- What you are signing is not what you intended.

These are all normal feelings. They will all soon dissipate, and then you can look back and smile about your early ASL awkwardness. Be patient. This is a new and different way of communicating, and acclimating to a sighted language takes time. Just dig in your heels, and go to it.

Which Hand Do I Use?

This is the most commonly asked question, and it is quite easy to answer. You will use your stronger and naturally dominant hand. This hand is the one you use daily while writing and eating and doing most tasks. Therefore, if you are right-handed, then your right hand will be your dominant signing hand. If you use your left hand for most daily tasks, then the left becomes your dominant signing hand.

For those novice signers who are ambidextrous, you'll need to choose one hand to be your dominant hand. If you're having trouble deciding, ask yourself the following questions:

- Which hand do I consistently use when writing and eating?
- Which hand do I use when tossing or catching a ball?
- Which hand do I use when reaching?
- Which hand has a natural feel when forming a sign?
- Which hand gives me an extended comfort zone?

As mentioned before, the new signer often feels very awkward and out of control. If you are a natural "righty" or "lefty," do not change your dominant action hand and arm simply because it feels a bit uncomfortable at the start. Give it some time—this feeling is normal and soon dissipates.

ALERT!

Once you have made the decision to be a right-handed or left-handed signer, do your absolute best not to switch back and forth. This point cannot be stressed strongly enough. Changing your dominant signing hand will only serve to confuse you as you acquire this new skill. This is especially true for new signers.

Some Signs Require Two Hands

Now that you have made your decision to sign with your right hand or left hand, we come to just a little curve in the road. Not all signs are formed using just one hand. Many signs require the use of both hands, and the use of the dominant hand does not always apply here. There are three different ways to form signs:

1.

One-handed signs are formed using only your dominant hand. Here's an example.
★ ★ ★

◀ **MIRROR:** Form the sign for "mirror" by imitating that you are holding a small vanity mirror and looking into it.

2.

Two-handed symmetrical signs require the use of both hands moving equally. Here's an example.
★ ★ ★

◀ **RAIN:** Form the sign for "rain" with your palms down, fingers spread, dropping your hands down several times to imitate rain.

3.

Two-handed asymmetrical signs require movement from the dominant, active hand while the other hand remains stationary or acts as the support base for the dominant hand. Here's an example.
★ ★ ★

◀ **SUNRISE, SUNSET:** To sign "sunrise," hold your stationary arm level and nearest to your chest. With your dominant hand, form the handshape of "O" and bring it upward to a high-noon position. Now, bring the arm back down level with the elbow of the stationary arm. This represents "sunset."

Look at these images and use the appropriate hand or hands to form the signs just as you see them demonstrated. Now, as a mini-drill, repeat forming these signs three times each. Repetition allows you to gain a feel for the hand and arm movement used in creating these signs. Each one of these three signs should feel quite different from the others as you execute it.

While this may seem a little confusing right now, don't worry yourself about it. As you move along and acquire vocabulary, one-handed, two-handed symmetrical, and two-handed asymmetrical signing will begin to have greater clarity.

You have signed "mirror" one-handed and "rain" two-handed, using the same movement/direction equally. You have signed "sunrise" and "sunset" using your dominant hand to create the action and movement, while your nondominant hand and arm remained stationary.

Strategies

You are fast approaching the chapters that will teach you signed vocabulary for ASL. As you go through the upcoming lessons, you'll gain a greater understanding and advance more rapidly if you put the following strategies into place:

- Practice, practice, practice; it is the magic key! Form the signs again and again, and set them to memory.
- Speed is not important. Sign slowly with clarity. The speed at which you sign will improve as you develop control. Clarity in forming signs far outweighs the importance of the speed at which they are delivered. Learn the signs well, and add the speed later.
- Learn to relax while signing. Keep your arms free and moving easily. You are not lifting weights in the gym. You are making signs flow through sight-waves. Always try to maintain a relaxed free flowing style.

- Take a sign language course, and it will enhance all the information that you find in these pages. A class, this book, *and* interactions with deaf family and friends will give you a jump-start into learning conversational ASL.
- Put aside your English grammar and the sound of words. Learn to think of words in terms of how they look, not how they sound.
- Use the signs you know by signing every chance you get. To really learn conversational ASL, you need to begin to associate within the Deaf community.

Eye Contact

Maintaining eye contact is a firm signing etiquette rule. Breaking eye contact during a signed conversation is considered extremely rude. Learn to develop attentive behaviors during signed conversations, such as nodding and adding an occasional signed exclamation, like "Yes," "Wow," or "Really," just as you would in an oral conversation. In addition, observing the signer's face at all times assists comprehension. Do not worry about focusing on the hands of the signer. Learn to see the whole picture, face and hands simultaneously. Remember, when you don't break that important eye contact, you show interest and respect for the signer. Keep in mind that eye contact is a two-way street. When you are the one doing signing, eye contact is still maintained.

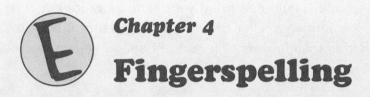

Chapter 4

Fingerspelling

Fingerspelling is the letter representation of each of the twenty-six letters of the alphabet. The use of fingerspelling is limited in ASL, only representing about 10 percent of the language's overall elements. It also has very specific rules. However, knowing and mastering the alphabet are very important when it comes to understanding the handshapes of signs.

Talking to Yourself

The palms of your hands must always face the receiver/reader when you are fingerspelling. If your palms are facing your chest, then you are talking to yourself, and the receiver cannot read the word or letters you are signing.

In addition, you should never turn your hand away, look at it to ensure you have formed a letter correctly, and then turn it back toward the reader. Rather than fingerspell to yourself, simply remember your palm should always face the receiver.

Becoming an Accurate Fingerspeller

In just a moment, you will be forming all the letters of the manual alphabet. But before we begin, you'll need to get into the proper position and learn special strategies to become a good fingerspeller. The following are tips to ensure accurate fingerspelling:

- Make sure your palm faces out toward the receiver/reader.
- Hold your dominant hand slightly to the right of your face and just below the chin.
- Make sure your elbow is close to your body.
- Practice fingerspelling with your elbow resting on a table or desk.
- Do not bounce the letters.
- Relax, and let the letters flow smoothly.
- Speed is not important; it is the clarity of the formation of each letter that matters.
- Do not say or mouth single letters.
- Move slightly to the right for double letters.

It takes time to get used to fingerspelling and to gain a comfort zone. Try to prevent developing the "bobber-weaver" syndrome and the famous "wing-thing." The "bobber-weaver" syndrome is when the signer fingerspells and moves his or her wrist and hand position, like a car weaving out of control. This pattern and flow is erratic, making it difficult to comprehend what is being fingerspelled. The "wing-thing" is when the signer, while fingerspelling, constantly lifts his or her elbow away from the body, as if about to take flight.

To help control and prevent the "bobber-weaver" and "wing-thing," here are a few tricks that you can learn. During an ASL conversation in which you fingerspell, use your left arm as a support for your right elbow. (If your left hand is dominant, then use your right for support.) This support position is the same as when you formed the signs for "sunrise, sunset" in Chapter 3. Another way to stabilize your hand and arm is to hold your wrist with your left hand, just below the wrist bone. This enables you to immediately feel when your fingerspelling becomes out of control or is starting to take flight. For the novice signer, another less obvious stabilizer is to place the left index finger on the front of the right wrist.

ALERT!

The images throughout this book show a right-handed signer. All images are presented with the model facing outward toward the receiver/reader. This means that you need to look at these just as if the person in the image is signing directly to you.

While practicing fingerspelling, try applying these small safeguards for that nice, steady, and smooth flow. Believe it or not, before you even realize it, you will not need to apply these fingerspelling safeguards at all. In the beginning, though, these serve as control mechanisms that serve the novice signer quite nicely.

Hand Warmup

You will be using your hands in a manner that you're not accustomed to. Therefore, to prevent any discomfort, it's a good idea to do some hand exercises and warmups. Okay, a one, a two, and a three!

1. Shake your hands briskly with your fingers parted.
2. Stretch your hand to an open-finger "five" position until you can feel the skin stretching between each finger.
3. Create a piano strum, starting with your pinky, and ending with your index finger.

Ready? Now, let's do the one-two-three exercise all over again. Shake it out one more time! Good! Now you are ready to form the handshapes of the letters of the manual alphabet.

The Manual Alphabet (A–F)

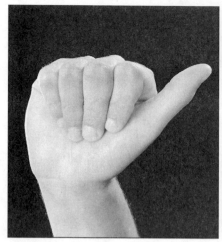

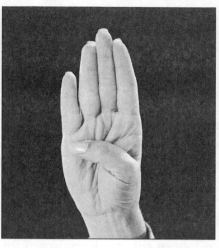

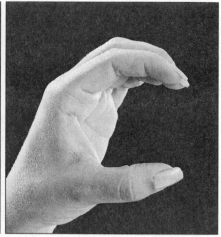

▲ **"A" HAND:** Closed fist with the thumb tucked against the side.

▲ **"B" HAND:** All fingers are vertical with the thumb in the palm.

▲ **"C" HAND:** Shape a "C" with all fingers neatly together. Palm should be facing left and opened slightly.

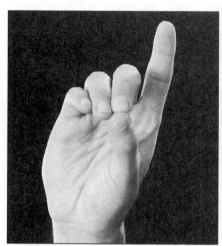

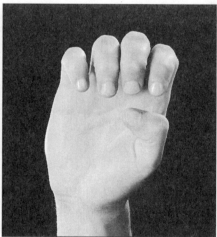

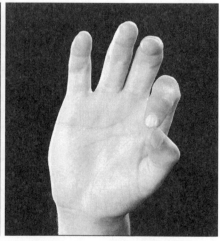

▲ **"D" HAND:** Place all fingers on the thumb, except for the index finger which should be in an upright, vertical position. Hint: Dump all your fingers on the thumb except the index finger. So remember, the next time you are practicing the letter "D," say the word "dump."

▲ **"E" HAND:** Pull all fingers back, with the thumb tucked into the palm.

▲ **"F" HAND:** Pinch the index finger to the thumb. The last three fingers are in a semi-vertical position.

Hint: Think of the last three fingers as a mini flag.

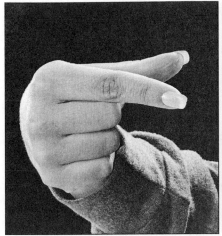

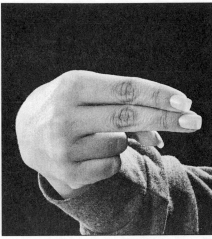

▲ **"G" HAND:** Hold the hand like a gun in the horizontal position, but with the trigger thumb down and tucked away.

▲ **"H" HAND:** Swing the forefinger and middle finger horizontally to the left, with the thumb down and tucked away.

▲ **"I" HAND:** Make a fist, and hold the pinky finger in the vertical position.

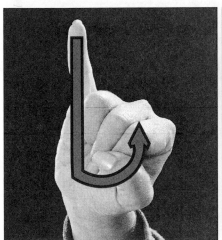

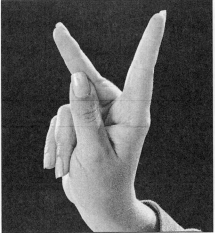

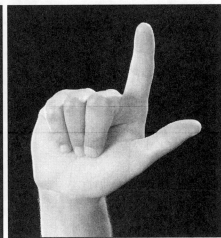

▲ **"J" HAND:** Using the same handshape as the letter "I," simply draw the "J" shape with the pinky finger.

▲ **"K" HAND:** Place the thumb between the index finger and the middle finger. Hold in an upright, vertical position. The last two fingers should be tucked into the palm and out of the way.

▲ **"L" HAND:** Make a fist, leaving the index finger in an upright, vertical position and the thumb sticking out.

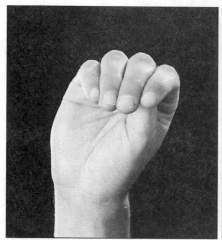

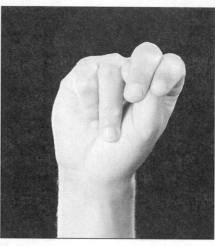

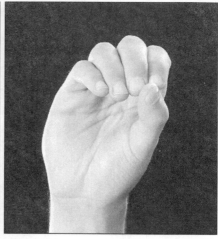

▲ **"M" HAND:** Wrap the first three fingers over the thumb.

▲ **"N" HAND:** Wrap the first two fingers over the thumb.

▲ **"O" HAND:** Form a nice round "O" by resting the index and middle fingers or all the fingers on the thumb.

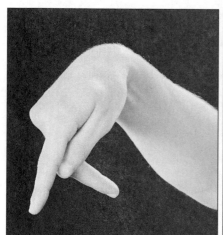

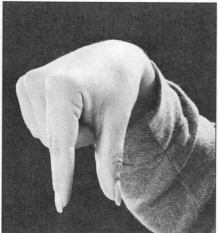

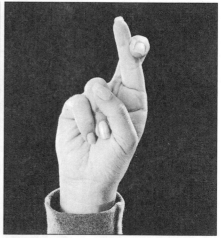

▲ **"P" HAND:** Place the thumb between the index finger and the middle finger. Tuck the last two fingers into the palm and out of the way. Drop your wrist so the middle finger and index finger are inverted and facing downward.

▲ **"Q" HAND:** Extend the thumb and the index finger downward, with the remaining fingers tucked away into the palm. Hint: The letter "Q" is made like the letter "G," but with the wrist dropped down.

▲ **"R" HAND:** Cross the index finger and the middle finger. All the other fingers are tightly tucked away.

The Manual Alphabet (S–X)

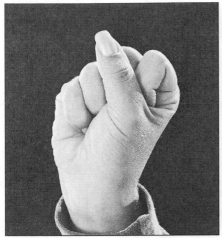

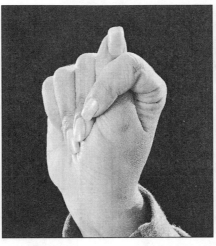

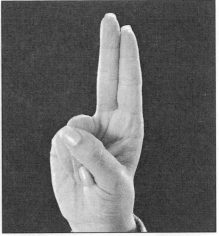

▲ **"S" HAND:** Make a fist with the thumb in front of the fingers. Hint: The letters "A" and "S" are easily confused. For "A," the thumb is on the side of the fist; for "S," the thumb is in front of the fist.

▲ **"T" HAND:** Tuck the thumb between the index finger and the middle finger.

▲ **"U" HAND:** The index finger and the middle finger are held together in the upright, vertical position, with the rest of the fingers tucked away.

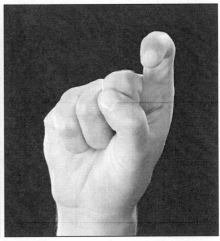

▲ **"V" HAND:** The index finger and the middle finger are spread open, creating a "V" and held in the upright, vertical position, with the rest of the fingers tucked away.

▲ **"W" HAND:** The index, middle, and ring finger are spread and held upright in the vertical position. Hold the pinky finger down with the thumb.

▲ **"X" HAND:** Make a fist with the thumb in front, leaving the index finger upright but bent into a hook shape.

The Manual Alphabet (Y–Z)

▲ **"Y" HAND:** Extend the thumb and the pinky finger with all other fingers tucked against the palm of the hand.

▲ **"Z" HAND:** Make a fist with the index finger extended in the horizontal position. Trace the "Z" shape in the air with your index finger.

Did you have the palm of your hand facing you at any time? If you did, then you were talking to yourself. Oops! Remember one of the first rules in fingerspelling: Palm always faces the receiver.

FACT

In 1620, Juan Pablo de Bonnet published the first book that illustrated a manual alphabet, entitled *The Simplification of the Letters of the Alphabet*.

Now, you need to repeat and practice the alphabet two more times. When you feel you have mastered the handshapes of the alphabet, then you will be ready to teach it to someone else. Perhaps that person will be a family member, friend, or a coworker. If you teach the alphabet to someone else, you will have a practice partner.

Practice Session #1

You're not done yet! There's still a lot of practice to be done before you are able to master fingerspelling. Using the following information, practice forming the letters by groups. Try memorizing the letters that are in each hand position.

- A, E, O, M, N, S, T, and Z are formed with a closed hand.
- B, C, D, F, I, J, K, L, R, U, V, W, X, and Y are formed in a vertical position.
- G and H are formed in a horizontal position.
- P and Q are formed open, inverted, and downward.

The handshapes of the letters of the alphabet vary in degrees from closed to open, horizontal to vertical, and inverted. In order to become comfortable and familiar with the handshapes and positions of the manual alphabet, you must practice, practice, practice!

The "I Love You" sign is one of the most popular slang signs and is easily recognized. The characteristics of this handshape are what bring forth the meaning. The pinky represents the letter "I." The index finger and extended thumb represent the "L" in "love." The combination of the pinky and the thumb extended represent the letter "Y" for "you."

◀ **I LOVE YOU:**
Combining the "I," "L," and "Y" forms the "I Love You" sign.

Practice Session #2

By now you should be starting to get the feel and look of the handshapes of the letters. Don't forget to do your hand warmups before each practice session! Here are some practice ideas to build your fingerspelling skills. Some of these practice ideas can be done right in your car. Fingerspell the following:

- Names of family
- Street and town names
- Things on the grocery list
- Names you see on trucks

The novice signer needs to see and feel these new, manual letters of the alphabet. Hopefully, you have been practicing and are acquiring the feel of each letter. Now you know how to make the shapes of the letters. Let's move on and find out when to use fingerspelling.

Proper Names

When you don't know a sign for a word, first try to describe it by acting it out, pointing, miming, or drawing it. In other words, don't use fingerspelling as your first choice when you don't know a sign. Fingerspelling is not a substitute for signing. In ASL, fingerspelling is only used approximately 10 percent of the time. Even then, it is only used for the following situations:

- Proper names
- Names of towns, cities, and states
- Specific brand names of products or services
- Titles of books and movies

As a word of caution, you should know that the letters "D" and "F" are constantly confused by new ASL students. Use these hints: *flag* for the letter "F" (think of the last three fingers as the stripes of a flag); and *dump* for the letter "D" (*dump* all your fingers on the thumb except for the index finger).

Spelling Bee

It is time to practice fingerspelling three-letter words. The movement from letter to letter will improve the agility of your fingers. Later, you and your fingerspelling partner can practice the spelling bee game together. Haven't found a partner yet? Well, do your best to locate one, and remember: To teach is to relearn.

The instructions for the spelling bee with a partner are as follows. Working from a list, each person alternately and randomly selects a word to fingerspell. The receiver must correctly fingerspell the word back to the sender. Each word is then checked off. Continue in this fashion until you have fingerspelled all the words. Try making the game a little more difficult. Create a new list of fifty words. This time, these words should be four to five letters in length. You can continue playing the spelling bee game in this same fashion by simply increasing the length and difficulty of the words.

Next, try this little twist on the game. This is similar to deaf/blind interpreting. This new twist is a terrific way to really adopt the feel of each letter. You can begin by using words from the same list, like the three-letter word chart presented here as a sample. This time, instead of looking at the letters, each person feels the handshapes of the letters. It begins by having your partner close their eyes while you fingerspell into the palm of your partner's hand. Your partner can use their free hand if they choose, to feel the entire shape of the letters. This version can be a lot of fun, so give it a try. You will be pleasantly surprised at how quickly you adapt to playing these interesting fingerspelling games. All the games suggested are a great way to practice mastering the alphabet. Don't forget that mastering the alphabet is an important first building block for the novice signer.

cat	mop	top	tap	nap
tip	bag	pit	hat	lip
mug	hit	sip	zip	lug
dim	pie	eye	hug	dye
sag	zap	cap	bit	but
wax	oar	not	get	fit
eat	jar	box	rat	six
van	gin	gym	sir	was
oat	fox	ear	jam	kit
raw	get	jaw	wet	nip

Initialized Signs

Initialized signs, also known as borrowed signs, are signs that—in general—borrow the first letter of words. The following practice exercise requires moving and placing the letters of the alphabet in specific locations on or around the body. This way, you create an initialized sign and, thus, a whole new word.

The Sign	The Letter
Attitude	Tap the "A" hand on the heart.
Boss	Tap the "B" hand on the heart.
Coach	Tap the "C" hand on the top of the right shoulder.
Dentist	Tap the "D" hand on the front teeth.
Elevator	Raise the "E" hand upward in front of the body.
Feather	Slide the "F" hand over the top of the ear.
Glasses	Stroke the "G" hand along the frame of an imaginary pair of glasses.
Hospital	Use the "H" hand to form a cross on the upper left arm.
Idea	Place the "I" hand on the corner of the eye and move forward slightly.
Jeans	Use the "J" hand while making the "J" motion on the right hip.
King	Tap the "K" hand on the left shoulder, then down on the right hip.
Loser	Place the "L" hand in the middle of the forehead.
Medical	Tap the "M" hand on the inside of the left wrist.
Nurse	Tap the "N" hand on the inside of the left wrist.
Opinion	Place the "O" hand on the temple and move forward slightly.
Prince	Tap the "P" hand on the left shoulder, then down on the right hip.
Queen	Tap the "Q" hand on the left shoulder, then down on the right hip.
Rose	Tap the "R" hand under each nostril.
South	Move the "S" hand straight down.
Toilet	Shake the "T" hand.
Uncle	Place the "U" hand on the temple.
Vegetable	Tap the "V" hand on each corner of the mouth.
Water	Tap the "W" hand just below the lower lip.
Xylophone	Tap both "X" hands alternately, imitating playing the xylophone.
Yellow	Shake the "Y" hand.
Zoo	Form the letters "Z," "O," and "O," while moving slightly to the right.

Fingerspelled Loan Signs

Another way the letters of the manual alphabet are used is in the application of fingerspelled loan signs. Fingerspelled loan signs have unique patterns and movement. They normally have two to five letters, and they are commonly used words. These words are all formed and shaped in various patterns, like so:

- "Bus" is fingerspelled using the letters "B" to "S" in a downward, vertical movement.
- "All" is fingerspelled using the letters "A" to "L" in a sweeping movement from left to right.
- "Dog" is fingerspelled using the letters "D" to "G" as if snapping the fingers.
- "Apt" is fingerspelled using the letters "A," "P," and "T," bending the wrist downward.
- "Refrigerator" is fingerspelled using the letters "R," "E," and "F" in a vertical downward motion.

The loan signs that you have just signed have been developed over a period of time and have proven to be an expedient way of signing these words. These "loan signs" truly, through time, have become whole ASL signs. As you move along in your study of sign language, and as you perhaps become involved with Deaf signers, many of the things that have been mentioned here will become fine-tuned. The magic word is "practice."

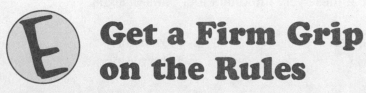

Chapter 5

Get a Firm Grip on the Rules

It is important to know the rules governing the proper use of sign language. The explanation of the rules called the "Big Four" will add clarity to the important elements in sign language. Additionally, in this chapter, you will be introduced to intonation, plurals, and a little bit of sign etiquette.

The Big Four

A sign is a unit of language that is formed with distinctive handshapes, locations, specific movements, and facial expressions. The signs have four independent parts. These parts play exacting roles, and if any one of them is changed, the meaning of the sign is altered. Let us take a close look at these very important four parts of signs:

1. Handshape

2. Location

3. Movement

4. Palm position

The term "handshape" refers to the specific shape of the hand while it is forming the sign. The handshapes could be the letters of the alphabet, a claw, an extended index finger, an "open five" hand, or a curved hand. Changing the handshape changes the meaning of a sign.

When we talk about "location," we mean the place where the sign is formed. The sign for "mother" and "father" have the same handshape, an "open five." However, the meaning is changed when that same handshape is placed in different locations. The location of these signs indicates the genders.

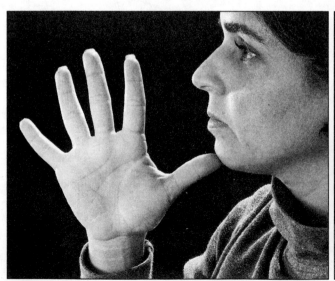
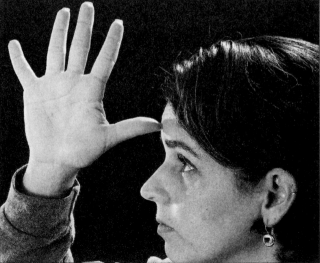

▲ **MOTHER:** The sign for mother is made on the chin.　▲ **FATHER:** The sign for father is made on the forehead.

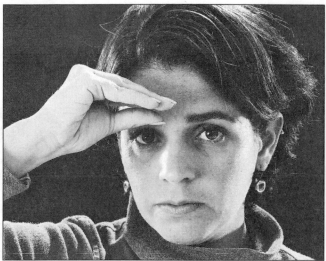

▲ **MALE:** All male signs are made from the forehead. (Hint: Think of tipping a hat.)

▲ **FEMALE:** All female signs are made from the jaw line. (Hint: Think of tying a bonnet.)

The term "movement" describes the action that makes the sign, such as moving in a circle, up and down, forward or backward. An example would be using the index finger and pointing upward. This movement forms the sign "up." Using the index finger and pointing downward, on the other hand, forms the sign "down." There are many signs just like the ones described, such as in/out and come/go. Simply changing the movement changes the meaning of the sign.

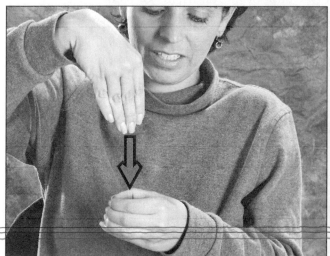

▲ IN

▲ OUT

The term "palm position" refers to the position of the palms of your hands and the direction the palm is facing. For example, placing your palm on your own chest would mean "mine." Facing your palm toward the reader would translate to "your."

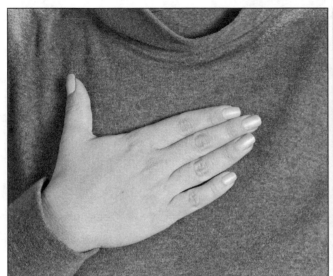

▲ **MINE:** To sign "mine," place your palm on your chest.

▲ **YOUR:** To sign "your," face your palm toward the reader.

These four rules of sign are very important elements of sign language. So let's take a moment to quickly review what you have learned. You have learned that the shape of your hand can change the meaning of a sign. In the previous chapter, you learned about initialized signs. In the practice, there was an instruction to tap the "A" hand on the heart to sign "attitude." However, if you changed the handshape to a "B" hand, the sign changed to "boss." It is a simple concept to remember: Change the handshape, and you change the meaning of the sign.

The second rule of sign is location. Once again, move the location—that is, where you are forming the sign—and the meaning is changed. The third rule is movement. Change any movement, and you form a completely different sign. The fourth rule is the palm position. When changed, this too alters the meaning of the sign.

Describing Hand Positions

Now let's take a quick look at the definitions and explanations of the hand positions. You will see some of these descriptive terms used in this book and others used in ASL dictionaries and instructional texts:

- "Horizontal" hands are parallel to the floor.
- "Vertical" hands are pointing upward.
- "Inverted" hands are pointing downward.
- "Inward" hands are held with palms toward the body.
- "Outward" hands are held with palms away from the body.
- "Palm toward palm" hands are held with palms facing each other.
- "Palm-to-palm" hands are held with palms applied to each other.
- "Prone" hands are held with palms down.
- "Supine" hands are held with palms up.
- "Tandem" hands are held one behind the other, in a line.

This information is presented to give you a sense of familiarity when you see new and unfamiliar descriptions for signs. Learning any language takes time. The more you are exposed to the terminology, the easier it will be.

Signing Space

The center of the chest is called the "sight line." The eyes can easily focus on the sight line and at the same time are able to focus on the face, facilitating lip reading and making it easier to observe facial expression.

The "signing area," which includes the sight line, is the area where the majority of the signs are formed. This space can be visualized as a pyramid in shape. It starts at the top of the signer's head, goes down past the shoulders, and ends with a horizontal line across the waist. Therefore, when reading signs, look at the person who is signing in that pyramid shape. Keep in mind that the sight line moves with the signer. If while you are signing, you should turn slightly left or right, the sight line will still be the center of your chest.

Reading signs can be tiring, and a signer must consider this. You can lessen eyestrain on the part of your reader by wearing solid-colored clothing. If you have been mulling the possibility of enrolling in an ASL course, keep this in mind. When you are preparing to attend the class, give your wardrobe a second look. It should be solid and free of design. In other words, don't wear sweatshirts with those huge logos in the middle of your sight line.

Intonation

Intonation in sign language is made through a variety of ways. A sign can be formed with intensity to show intonation. For instance, if you worked hard all day, you might sign "work" by striking the "S" hands together with force.

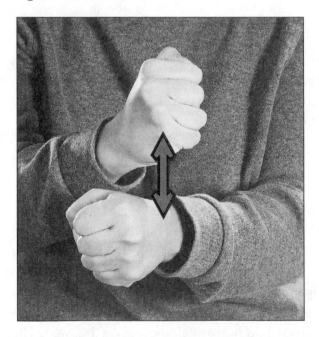

◄ **WORK:** To sign "work," strike the "S" hands twice.

Another way to show intonation is to execute a sign with varying degrees of speed. If you were signing you had to go somewhere in a hurry, you would sign that with a quick snapping motion. On the other hand, if you were just taking a nice slow drive, you would sign that slowly, with the appropriate casual facial expression. Another way of expressing intonation is by using facial expression along with intensity and motion. These elements play an important role in conveying your meaning.

FACT

The longer you sign, the better your skill will become at adding intonation, denotation, and strong visual inflections that enhance your signs. As with all things, these elements just take time and practice to be applied appropriately.

For example, if you want to express you love something you would sign "love" by gently crossing your arms over your chest. However, if you are madly in love with something or someone, then you would make the same sign tightly, hugging your chest and perhaps rocking back and forth and adding a big delightful smile. These movements, along with your facial expression, instantly add a strong degree to the word "love."

◄ **LOVE:** To sign "love," cross both arms and hug the chest. This sign can be formed with either closed fists or open palms.

Sign Etiquette

Earlier we discussed the signer's space. A question that is often asked is, "How do I pass through the space between two signers?" The answer is to avoid passing between the signers if at all possible. If it is unavoidable, you simply sign, "excuse," while you quickly walk between the two signers.

◀ **EXCUSE:** To sign "excuse," stroke the "flat" hand on the left "open" palm several times.

Another question that is often asked is, "How do you get the attention of the deaf?" There are several different ways:

- Tap lightly on a shoulder.
- Wave a hand.
- Flash the lights on and off.
- Stomp on the floor.
- Rap or tap on the surface of a table.

Tapping on a shoulder and waving are the first two preferred ways for getting the attention of the deaf. Please keep in mind that when flashing the lights or stomping on the floor, these would be executed in moderation. If the lights are flashed continuously and rapidly, it could be interpreted as an emergency. The same applies for stomping the feet on the floor. In addition, try to avoid nervously strumming on a table if you are with a group of deaf or hard of hearing people. This type of behavior could be distracting. Also, chewing gum and long decorated nails only serve as distractions when signing.

Plurals

There are many different ways to pluralize signs in ASL. Some of the methods are very simple, while others require the use of classifiers and numbers. (You will find classifiers described in Chapter 7, and numbers in Chapter 8.) The easiest way to pluralize a sign is to make the sign two or more times. For instance, the sign for tree, when reduplicated, becomes forest. The sign for child, when made multiple times, becomes children. The following are ways to pluralize:

- **A "sweep":** A signer can use the index finger and "sweep" across the front to indicate a multiple number, such as "they" or "them," or a flock.
- **Numbers:** Sign the object or thing and add the numbers.
- **Quantifiers:** Sign the object or thing and add signs such as many, several, or few.
- **Classifiers:** Sign the object or thing incorporating classifiers, which demonstrate shape, group, and quantity.

Sign Order

ASL syntax—that is, sign order—is often difficult to master during the early part of the process of acquiring signing skills. The syntax when signing generally follows this order: object, subject, verb. Time, if applicable, is signed at the beginning of the sentence and often signed again at the end of the sentence. However, ASL syntax is often varied in short sentences. It also varies regionally. For instance, the order could be seen as subject, verb, object. This is made with modifications, including omitting any "to be" verbs.

FACT

Deaf people rarely leave a room without an explanation, such as getting a drink or going to the bathroom. When a deaf person suddenly leaves a room without an explanation, it is considered rude.

These sign orders may sound peculiar to you. Based on this reason alone, you are encouraged to enroll in a sign language course and try to meet and socialize with members of the Deaf community. It will be a little while before the reasons for the syntactical order of ASL become clear and fall into place. The transition does occur much more quickly when you begin to see language instead of hearing language.

Since this transition takes a while, you can continue to work on sharpening your skills at getting your hands under control, recognizing hand shapes, maintaining eye contact, and acquiring sign vocabulary. Speaking of vocabulary, as you've probably guessed, there is much more in store for you. Learning the rules to any language is difficult. Stay focused, maintain your interest, and keep up the good work. The more you know, the easier it gets.

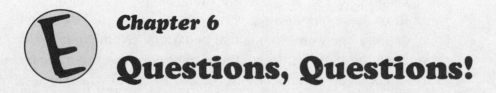

Chapter 6

Questions, Questions!

Our daily conversations are filled with questions. Therefore, in order to communicate effectively using ASL, you'll need to learn how to ask and receive questions. This chapter will teach you to form questions and apply them with appropriate facial expressions.

Two Groups of Questions

The strong visual aspects of sign language require us to divide questions into two categories. The first category is the "wh- words": who, what, when, where, why, which, and how. Questions that use these words ask for specific information. The second category is "yes-no" questions. These are questions that can be answered with a simple yes or no.

Both of these question types need to be supported by specific facial expressions with "nonmanual behaviors." Nonmanual behaviors do not use the hands. Instead, these behaviors use the eyes, facial expressions, head movement, body posture, or body language. Signers use nonmanual behaviors to show emotion, emphasize a point, make a negative statement, and ask questions. Facial expressions are equal to vocal intonation. When you do not apply the proper facial expressions and nonmanual behaviors, your questions may not be interpreted correctly.

Applying Nonmanual Behaviors

As a novice signer, your first step toward acquiring the important elements of facial expressions and nonmanual behaviors begins right here, with the two categories of questions. Your first attempts will feel awkward. Be assured that this feeling is quite normal. The skill of applying facial expression and nonmanual behaviors will gradually build and develop naturally as you further your studies in sign language. Keep in mind that you are in the early chapters of this book. There will be many chances for you to build in your skills in sign language.

"Wh-" Word Questions

When asking a wh- word question, do the following:

- Furrow your eyebrows together.
- Tilt your head forward.
- Make direct eye contact.
- Hold your last sign, usually a wh- word.

When asking a wh- word question, it is common to sign the wh-word at the beginning and repeat it at the end of the question. The wh-word at the end will be the sign that is held with eyebrows furrowed, head tilted, and direct eye contact maintained. In English, the ASL for one of these questions would sound something like this: "Where restroom where?"

Yes-No Questions

When asking a "yes-no" question, do the following:

• Raise your eyebrows to widen your eyes.
• Tilt your head slightly forward.
• Make direct eye contact.
• Hold the last sign in your sentence.

◄ **QUESTION MARK:** Occasionally, a "yes-no" question is accompanied by a question mark. To add a question mark, use the index finger and trace a question mark.

Answering Questions

It's not enough to just be able to ask questions. You'll also need to know how to answer them, or the conversation will be one-sided!

▲ **YES:** When answering "yes" to a question, shake the "S" hand up and down, and use a nod of affirmation.

▲ **NO:** When answering "no" to a question, bring the extended thumb, index, and middle fingers together and include a shake of the head. The sign for "no" is small, and, at times, it can be easily missed. A negative headshake ensures your answer is understood.

Review Handshapes

Before we begin to learn additional vocabulary, you need to become comfortable with the handshapes of the alphabet. Take a minute now and sign the alphabet in order to refresh these handshapes in your mind. Throughout this book, the directions on how to form signs will refer to handshapes, such as the "D" hand or "F" hand. These instructions are simply describing a handshape and, generally, there is minimal association with the letter value. When there is an association, these signs will be referred to as "initialized signs" or "loan signs."

Signing Wh- Words

Now it's time to sign the wh- words with the appropriate facial expressions. Get ready, eyebrows down and furrowed, head tilted, and here we go!

Signing Wh- Words

▲ **WHO:** To sign "who," use the index finger and circle the mouth.

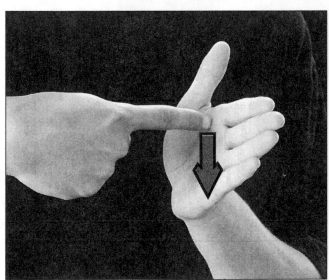

▲ **WHAT:** To sign "what," draw the index finger of the "D" hand down the left "open" palm. Another way is to simply shrug with palms facing upward.

▲ **WHEN:** To sign "when," the index finger of the right "D" hand circles clockwise around the index finger of the left "D" hand.

Signing Wh- Words

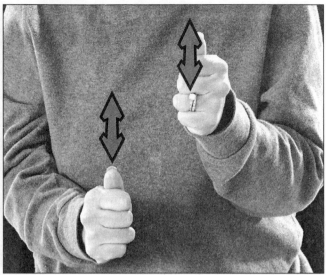

▲ **WHERE:** To sign "where," repeatedly shake the index finger of the "D" hand right to left.

▲ **WHICH:** To sign "which," move the "A" hands alternately up and down.

▲ **WHY:** To sign "why," place the fingertips on the temple and pull down, forming into the "Y" hand.

Signing Wh- Words

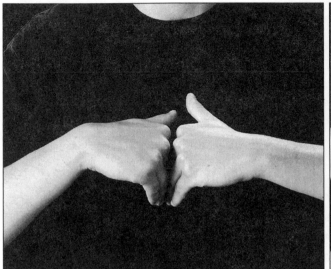

▲ **HOW:** To sign "how," touch the knuckles of both "curved" hands in front of the chest and rotate hands upward together ending with the palms up.

Sign Variations

Throughout the upcoming chapters, you will be shown sign variations. Many of these variations come from regional differences. Sign variations also occur when older signs are reformatted to improve their delivery and, in turn, to make them more expedient. New signs are also developed in order to keep pace with technological advances.

In general, just as with all languages, normal changes occur over time. Therefore, please be aware that the images shown throughout this book are basic signs. In order to be a good signer, you must be flexible and understand that there can be a variety of ways to form a sign.

You need to be aware of important variations for two wh- words. The variation of the "who" sign is a commonly used sign. Use the "L" hand and place the thumb in the cleft of the chin, then flick the index finger. The other variation is that for "why." Use an "open five" hand, with the middle finger slightly lowered, and touch the side of the head. Then pull away while wiggling the middle finger.

The Interview

During your sign language journey, chances are good that you will meet a member of the Deaf community. You will need to be prepared to answer a few questions. It is natural and considered a part of the culture for a member of the Deaf community to ask you several questions. The reason for these many questions is to establish a connection back to the Deaf community. In just a moment, we will go through an interview exercise in which you will sign both questions and answers to those questions. But first, you need to add a few vocabulary words to your growing list.

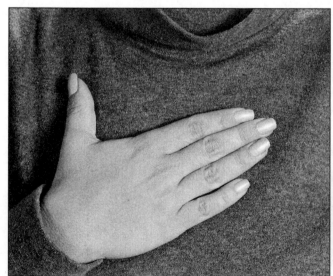

▲ **MY:** To sign "my," place the open palm on your chest.

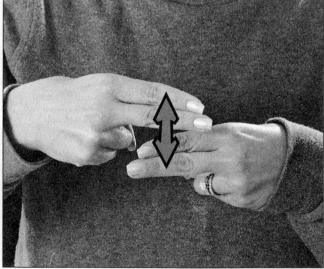

▲ **NAME:** To sign "name," cross and tap the "H" hands twice.

The Interview

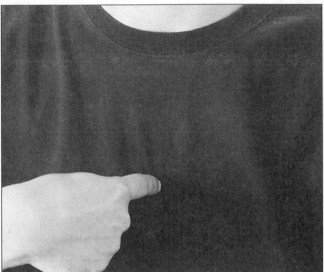

▲ **I, ME:** To sign "I" or "me," use the index finger to point to yourself.

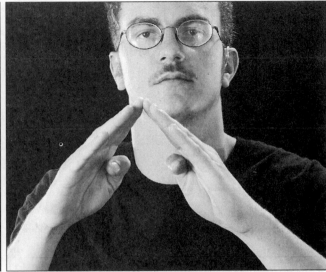

▲ **HOUSE:** To sign "house," touch the fingertips of the "flat" hands, imitating the roof of a house.

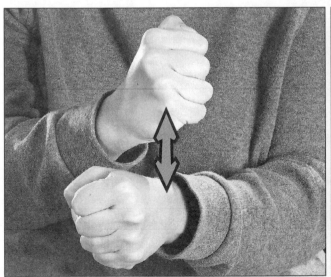

▲ **WORK:** To sign "work," strike the "S" hands twice. Remember, intonation can be applied within this sign by striking the "S" hands together with force multiple times.

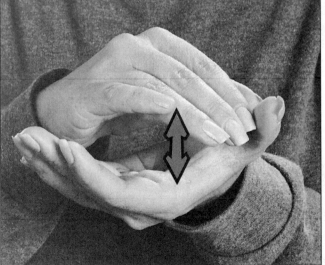

▲ **SCHOOL:** To sign "school," clap hands twice.

The Interview

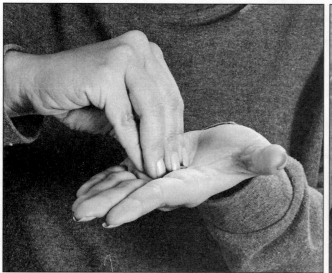 

▲ **LEARN:** To sign "learn," place all the fingertips into the left palm. Next, pull upward with a modified "O" hand and place it on the forehead, with an action that suggests putting knowledge in the mind.

Practice an Interview

Looking at the following interview, you will notice that the questions are written in an approximate sign order. This order demonstrates that the wh- word is signed at the beginning and then repeated at the end of the question. The responses are also presented in a simple sign order. At first, this sign order will sound strange to your auditory ear. You must keep in mind that sign language is a *visual* language. Therefore, how it sounds grammatically is not relative to the way it is received through the eyes. The signs are perfectly acceptable in the order they are signed.

You will need to look at the previous wh- words and connect them with the additional vocabulary presented. All these signs need to be accompanied with appropriate facial expressions and nonmanual behaviors.

Question	Response
What name what?	My name (fingerspell name).
Where live where?	I live (fingerspell town).
Where work where?	My work (fingerspell workplace).
Where school where?	My school (fingerspell school name).
Where learn ASL where?	I learn ASL (fingerspell location).

You have just learned how to sign everyday questions and responses! Don't let the English order and sound of these sentences concern you. Signing "my name" without the word "is" is perfectly acceptable. The word "is" is incorporated in the dimensional movement, so a separate sign would be redundant.

Learning sign order, facial expressions, and nonmanual behaviors is a skill that develops slowly with practice and experience. At this point, your primary focus is learning to form the signs accurately, while gradually figuring out how to apply these additional elements. In order to do this, you will need to practice signing these questions and responses the way they have been written in the preceding example.

FACT

If you answer that you have a deaf family member or childhood friend, be prepared to provide information regarding the school they attended and the year of their graduation. Deaf people consider school as their home. Since most of these students lived at schools, fellow students are an extension of their family.

It is important to begin to develop a comfort level. As mentioned earlier, a member of the Deaf community may ask many questions to establish a connection. In doing so, you may be asked these additional questions: Do you have a deaf family member? Why are you learning sign language? Who is your teacher? Regardless of whether you ever have the experience of meeting a member of the Deaf community, you will still need these common, everyday question signs.

Rhetorical Questions

The facial expressions and nonmanual behaviors used when asking a rhetorical question include raising the eyebrows and tilting the head to the side and back. However, rhetorical questions are not true questions, and a response is not expected. It is the signer's intention, immediately following this type of question, to supply the answers and information. Rhetorical questions are commonly used in ASL and in the Deaf community. Using this type of question allows a signer to quickly get the attention of others and to introduce a new subject or information.

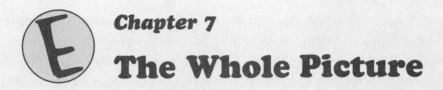

Chapter 7

The Whole Picture

Facial expressions are an important element of ASL. This chapter introduces this element with images for you to view and learn. Body language will be discussed, and we will introduce classifiers as well. All of these elements serve to build your skills toward becoming a well-rounded and knowledgeable signer.

A Face Is Worth a Thousand Signs

Facial expressions make a world of difference not only in sign language but also in everyday conversations. A simple frown or a tilt of the head can change or enhance conversations. In sign language, facial expressions are a part of nonmanual behaviors. In other words, they are not signs.

You can compare nonmanual behaviors to a person's mannerisms. These types of mannerisms simply happen and one doesn't think about them to produce them. The novice signer often has difficulty applying facial expressions and nonmanual behaviors because at first they seem extreme. However, if you were to videotape a natural conversation, you would see that facial expressions occur throughout a conversation.

For example, consider the case of a friend telling you that another friend had been in a car accident. Your reply might be, "What! Is he okay?" Your natural expression for "What!" would likely be a look of shock. Your eyes would widen, and your head could tip forward or back. The second part, "Is he okay?" might be accompanied by an expression of concern. These types of everyday facial expression occur naturally. In other words, to form these facial expressions is no big deal! You already know them, and you apply them constantly without even giving them a second thought.

ALERT!

In sign language, if you do not apply or possess facial expressions, you are considered a boring signer. Lack of facial expression is the ASL equivalent of speaking in a monotone.

In the previous chapter, you were introduced to facial expressions that accompanied the wh- words. Now, it's time to take a bigger step and enhance your awareness of applying appropriate facial expressions for other signs. View the following images, and note the facial expressions of the model. Then give it a try. Remember, you already know how to smile, frown, or look grouchy. The goal with these images is to sign each one with the appropriate facial expressions.

Facial Expressions

▲ **HAPPY:** To sign "happy," pat the chest upward several times and smile.

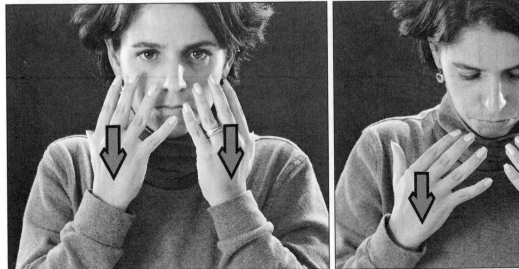

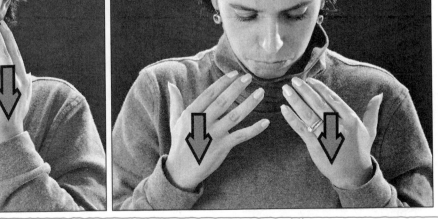

▲ **SAD:** To sign "sad," drop the "open five" hands from the face, while dropping the head and looking sad.

Facial Expressions

▲ **SORRY:** To sign "sorry," circle the "A" hand at the heart.

▲ **CRY, TEAR:** To sign "cry" or "tear," draw the index finger down the cheek beneath the eye several times. Both hands can be used, adding depth to the sign.

▲ **GROUCHY:** To sign "grouchy," bend and unbend curved "five" hands several times in front of face.

▲ **CRAZY:** To sign "crazy," pivot the curved "five" hand several times at the side of the head. Both hands may be used for this sign.

Facial Expressions

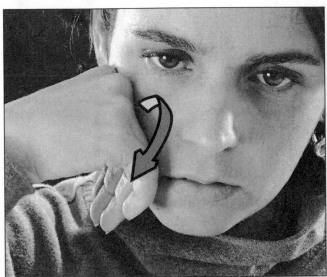

▲ **ASHAMED, SHAME, SHY:** To sign "ashamed," "shame," or "shy," brush the back of the fingers of a bent hand against the cheek in a forward arc movement.

▲ **JEALOUS:** To sign "jealous," twist pinky at mouth.

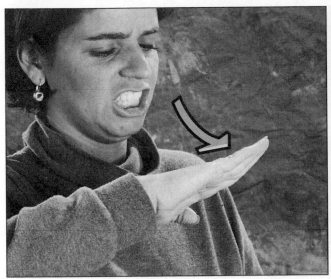

▲ **BAD:** To sign "bad," place the "B" hand palm down on the chin and toss the hand downward. Notice the facial intensity of "bad." Wow! That signer is conveying *very* bad!

▲ **GOOD:** To sign "good," place the "B" hand to the chin, then bring the "B" hand down and place it in the left palm.

Lean into It with Body Language

Everyone likes a story, and people love to tell their own. Children adore listening to and watching stories. If you want to become a good storyteller, use appropriate animated facial expressions, body language, and mime. In addition, you can use role-playing methods.

Role-Playing Using Facial and Body Language

As an example, let's imagine that your story has two characters, one on your left and one on your right. Simply apply a body shift to represent the position of these characters. To body shift, all you need to do is turn your torso. Let us imagine that your story characters are Shrek and the Princess. In order to demonstrate these characters, put Shrek on the right and Princess on the left. When you turn your torso to the right, adopt Shrek's character with a big upright chest puffed out. When you turn left, adopt a soft sweet feminine posture.

Throughout your story use appropriate eye gaze that models the characters' perspectives. For instance, when Shrek speaks to the Princess, make sure you are looking left with the appropriate eye gaze for his character. Without even realizing it, your facial and body language can convey a concept: Shrek's infatuation with the lovely Princess. The secret is in the eyes—blink repeatedly, fluttering your eyelashes while slightly swaying back and forth.

Storytelling with Style

If you are a professional who works with young children, have children of your own, or have friends who like to have fun, try imitating two characters in the manner described. Your audience will be delighted with this type of visual enhancement. When you first begin to practice role-playing, you don't even need to sign. Just start by enhancing your storytelling with body shifts, body mannerisms, appropriate facial expressions, and eye gazes. Soon, you will be taking a bow and doing an encore.

Using Signs in Storytelling

The following signs are easily applied in storytelling. Don't forget to use appropriate facial expressions.

Using Signs in Storytelling

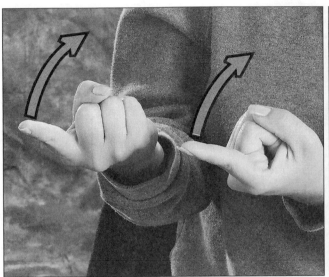

▲ **COME:** To sign "come," move the index fingers of the "D" hands toward you in a beckoning motion.

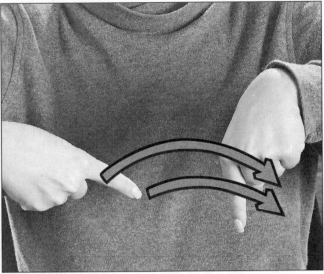

▲ **GO:** To sign "go," move the index fingers of the "D" hands away from the body.

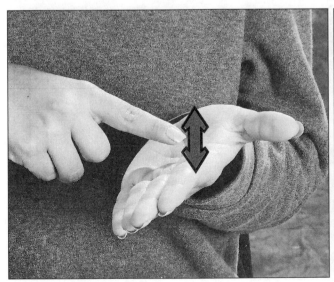

▲ **DISCUSS, ARGUE:** To sign "discuss" or "argue," strike the index finger of the "D" hand onto the left palm several times. Strike the palm with force for "argue."

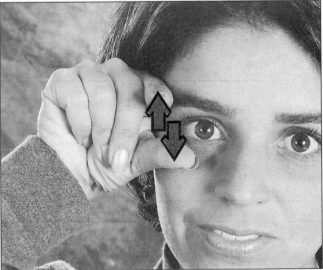

▲ **WAKE UP:** To sign "wake up," open the "G" hand at the side of the eye, imitating eyes opening.

Using Signs in Storytelling

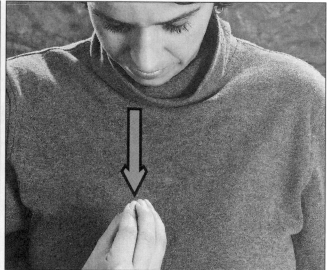

▲ **SLEEP:** To sign "sleep," place the "open five" hand in front of the face. Draw the fingers down and into a modified "O" hand.

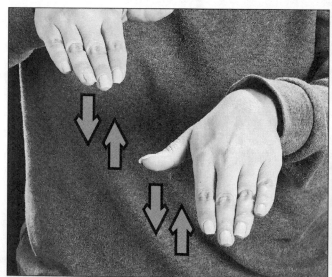

▲ **WALK:** To sign "walk," use the "flat" hands, with palms facing down, and move the hands alternately, imitating walking.

▲ **RUN:** To sign "run," use the modified "C" hands. Hold the right index finger on the left thumb and then move hands forward quickly while flicking the index finger and thumb.

Using Signs in Storytelling

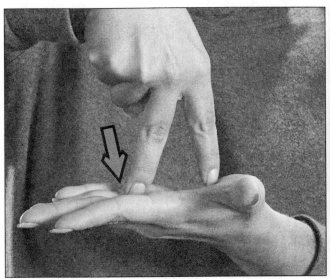

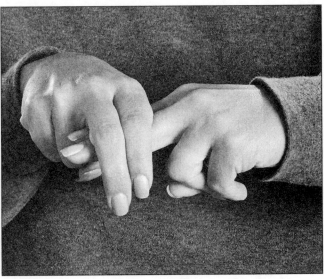

▲ **STAND:** To sign "stand," place the index and middle fingertips into the left open palm, imitating legs.

▲ **SIT:** To sign "sit," place the right "N" fingers over the extended left "N" fingers, imitating legs dangling.

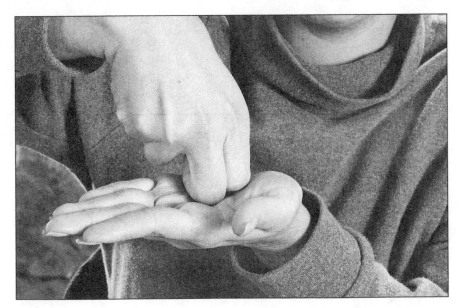

▲ **KNEEL:** To sign "kneel," place the knuckles of the "N" fingers into the open left palm.

Using Signs in Storytelling

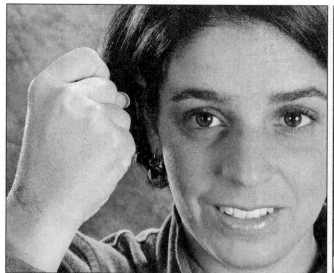 

▲ **UNDERSTAND:** To sign "understand," place the "S" hand at the temple and then snap open the index finger.

▲ **IN:** To sign "in," place the fingertips of "B" hand into left "O" hand.

▲ **OUT:** To sign "out," pull the fingertips of "B" hand out of left "O" hand.

Using Signs in Storytelling

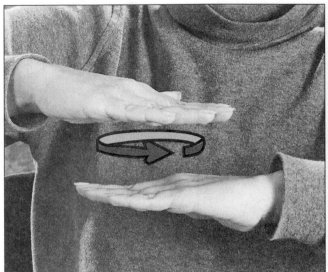

▲ **OVER:** To sign "over," move the right "flat" palm in a counterclockwise circle over left hand.

▲ **UNDER:** To sign "under," move the right "A" hand in a counterclockwise circle under left palm.

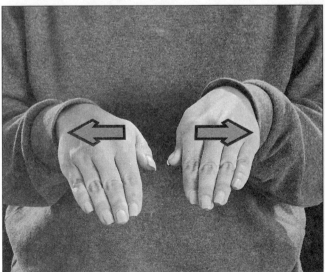

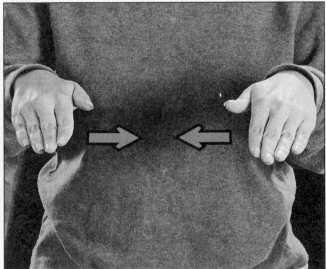

▲ **OPEN:** To sign "open," move the "flat" hands apart, imitating opening.

▲ **CLOSE:** To sign "close," move the "flat" hands together, imitating closing.

Using Signs in Storytelling

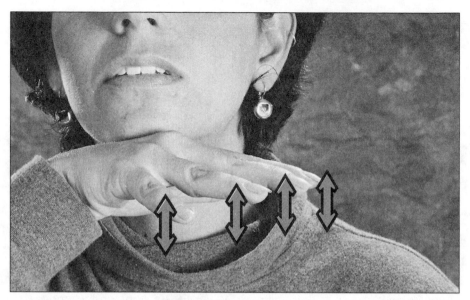

▲ **DIRTY:** To sign "dirty," wiggle four fingers under the chin.

▲ **FEAR:** To sign "fear," use the "S" hands opening to "five" hands.
The sign for fear can be enhanced by showing intensity on the face,
depending upon the degree of fear.

Classifiers, the Powerful Tool

Hopefully, you are learning that you can have fun while learning about sign language and its many elements along with the signed vocabulary. Now we will add yet another sign element to your new skills.

Classifiers are handshapes that can represent either a noun and its location and action (such as a car involved in a wreck) or a description of a noun (such as shape or size). There are a vast number of classifiers that demonstrate groups, shapes, sizes, and movement of objects. We're just going to scratch the surface of this subject by presenting a few easily applied classifiers.

ALERT!

Be aware that a sign does not exist for every word. Classifiers, when used correctly, can represent these words through shape and placement in a creative and clear manner. Another option would be to point to the item, when possible.

Classifiers are a powerful tool when used in storytelling, and they are very expedient in signed conversations. A signer will use one or two hands as needed when forming and applying classifiers. Novice signers are taught to form the actual sign first, then apply the classifier representation of that sign. Confused? Don't worry; we'll go over a few examples to help you understand.

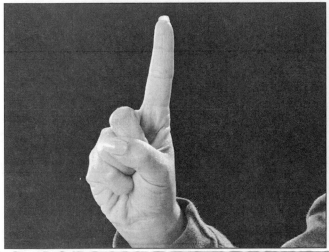

▲ This classifier represents thin long things, such as telephone poles or people. It is formed with the vertical index finger.

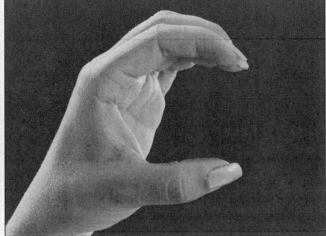

▲ This classifier represents cylindrical items, such as a glass or cup. It is formed with the handshape of "C."

Classifiers

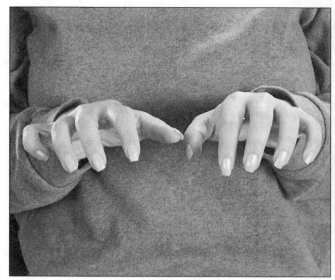

▲ This classifier represents a mass, such as piles, clumps, or buildings. It is formed with the "claw" handshape.

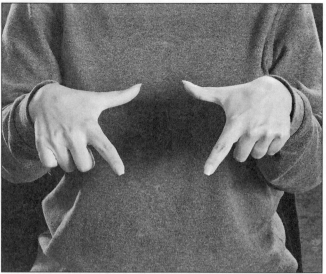

▲ This classifier represents round, flat, thin objects. It is formed with bent "L" handshapes.

The next classifier is used frequently. It represents flat objects, such as paper, walls, or floors, and is formed with a "flat" handshape. You will note there are three different images of the "flat" hand, in various positions.

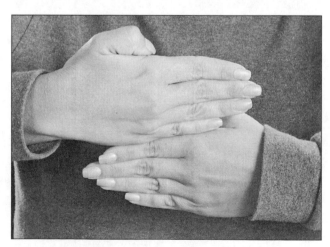

▲ First classifier representing flat objects.

Classifiers

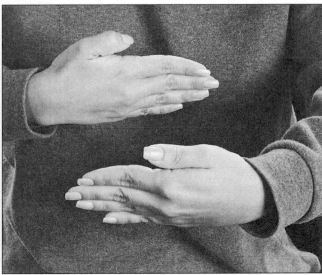

▲ Second classifier representing flat objects.

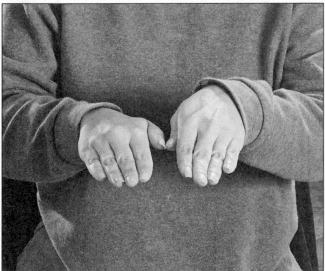

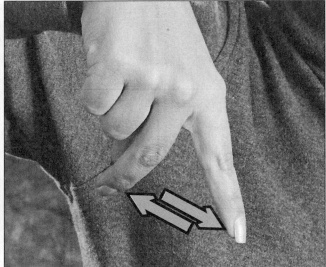

▲ Third classifier representing flat objects.

▲ This classifier represents the legs of a person. It is formed with an inverted "V" handshape.

Mold It, Shape It

You have examined the illustrations and made the handshapes of the classifiers. Congratulations! Now we're going to take a look at all the different ways you can use those handshapes. The following table shows a list of items beneath their appropriate classifier. These items can be easily pictured in your mind. Using classifiers, you can form these shapes as big or as small as you desire. You can move and arrange them anywhere within your signing space.

Flat hand	Claw hand	"C" hand	Bent "L"	Index finger
box	snowball	glass	plate	tree
table	light bulb	flashlight	pizza tray	thermometer
book	flowerbed	cup	cookie	stripes
floor	bushes	bowl	badge	telephone pole
ceiling	rubbish	vacuum hose	coaster	person
curtains	piles	vase	saucer	popsicle

Remember, some of these items require you to use two hands when shaping them with classifiers. Don't worry about grasping all the concepts of signing right now; it is, after all, just the beginning of your journey into the world of ASL. There is much more to come. Ⓔ

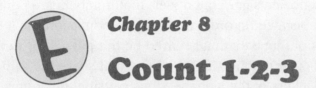

Chapter 8

Count 1-2-3

This chapter will introduce simple numbers and give you a guideline to master the basic formations. You will learn to form signed numbers with ease and quickly be counting up to a million on one hand. Along the way, you'll also learn how to sign fractions and signs related to money.

It's All in the Numbers

We use many different kinds of numbers in our daily conversation. For instance, a conversation might include a phone number, credit card number, model number, and so forth. Now it's time for you to learn how to use numbers in ASL.

Unfortunately, a novice signer often feels that numbers are confusing and somewhat complicated. In order to minimize confusion, we'll take a look at examples of numbers that seem to be the pitfalls for new signers. These particular numbers are the ones that share the same handshapes as the letters of the alphabet, thus causing the confusion. Don't become discouraged. There are only a few of these numbers, and there will be a guide for you. The context of a conversation generally adds the clarity that is needed to distinguish between a signed number and letter.

FACT

The way numbers are signed can vary according to region. In some regions, the numbers are signed with the palms facing you; in others, the palm is facing the reader. Don't let this worry you. Both palm positions are correct, depending on your geographical region and, perhaps, on your ASL teacher as well.

Your flexibility as a new signer really counts in this chapter. Tips and visual examples are right here to support you. Now, warm up your fingers and wrists and get ready to count to ten.

Counting to Ten

Counting to ten is easy. You have been doing this since you were a child. In this case, however, there is one little difference. When you were a child, you had to use two hands to count this high. In sign language, you can count to ten (and much higher) using just one hand! A nice starting place for the material we cover in this chapter is to learn to sign "number."

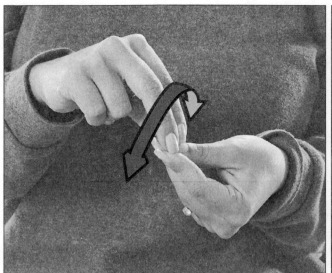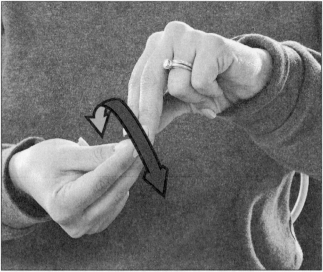

▲ **NUMBER:** To sign "number," touch the fingertips of both flattened "O" hands, and pivot back and forth alternately.

One Through Five

Now we can begin the simple task of counting to ten. The ASL form for counting is just a little different from the way you counted to ten as a child. With a quick look at the images, you should be able to duplicate the individual handshape of numbers one through five without any problems whatsoever. Keep in mind that the number three requires the vertical extension of your thumb along with your index and middle fingers. The handshape for the number five is referred to as the "open five."

Six Through Nine

The counting process changes for six through nine. It's easy; you only need to touch a specific finger to your thumb. Just think; there is no need to use both hands to count above five again!

One Through Five

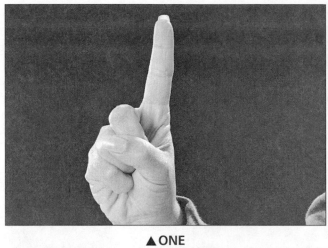

▲ ONE

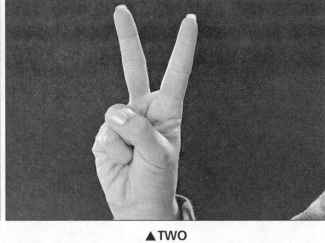

▲ TWO

▲ THREE

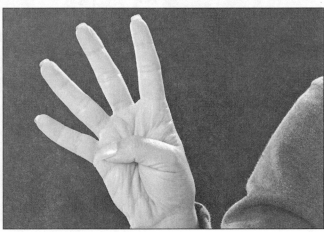

▲ FOUR

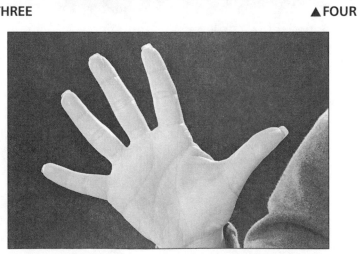

▲ FIVE

Six Through Ten

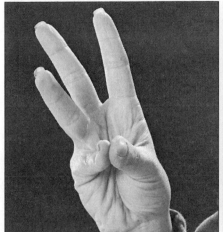

▲ **SIX:** To sign "six," touch the pinky finger to the thumb. If you're thinking that the number six looks like the letter "W," you're right. Remember, the context of a signed conversation will help you to differentiate between numbers and letters.

▲ **SEVEN:** To sign "seven," touch the ring finger to the thumb.

▲ **EIGHT:** To sign "eight," touch the middle finger to the thumb.

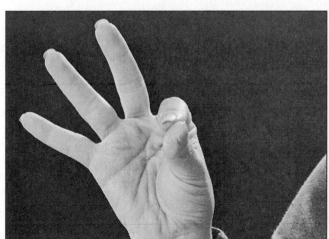

▲ **NINE:** To sign "nine," touch the index finger to the thumb. If you're thinking that the number "nine" is another example of duplicity, you're right again. It has the same handshape as the letter "F."

▲ **TEN:** To sign "ten," use the extended "A" hand and pivot the wrist to the right.

Time to Review

You made it to ten counting on one hand! Let's do a quick review of how you accomplished this. In sign language, the pinky finger represents the number six. The ring finger represents the number seven. The middle finger represents the number eight. The index finger represents the number nine. When you lightly touch any of these four fingers separately to the thumb, this action confirms the number position. Simply refer to this table until you master the numbers.

Number	Finger position
6	pinky
7	ring
8	middle
9	index
10	thumb

Now, let's examine those numbers and letters that share the same handshapes and that are the cause of some confusion for novice signers:

- The number "two" is formed in the same way as the letter "V."
- The number "six" is formed in the same way as the letter "W."
- The number "nine" is formed in the same way as the letter "F."
- The number "ten" is formed in the same way as the letter "A," but with the addition of a twist of the wrist.

Number Handshapes as Descriptors

You will find that the handshapes of numbers are also used as descriptors. Instructions in sign language dictionaries often refer to numbers to describe handshapes. For example, you may see entries that tell you to use the "one" hand or to use the "three" hand. In previous pages of this book, you have already read instructions on forming a sign that used the handshape of a number: an "open five" hand. Knowing how to form all the handshapes, including numbers, is a very important part of your new journey into this visual language.

Conversations with Letters and Numbers

When a conversation occurs that requires both letters and numbers, such as a password or an e-mail address, the dilemma can be resolved in two easy ways. The first resolve is to slightly shake the numbers back and forth while maintaining a smooth flow for the letters. This slight movement helps to establish that you are signing a number and not a letter. The second solution is to sign all numbers with the palm facing you and all letters with the palm facing the reader. Of these two methods, the first one, shaking the numbers, is the easiest for the novice signer.

As mentioned earlier, numerology in sign language has many different variations. Simply master the basic numbers, and you will successfully get through any conversations requiring signed numbers. Remember, stay flexible, because numbers change.

Tackling Eleven Through Nineteen

Now it's time to move on and learn the next section of numbers. As a memory guide to help you along, we'll refer to the numbers eleven through fifteen as the "flicks." (You'll see why in just a moment.) These numbers are formed with the palm facing you. Look back at the images of one through five, and set them in your mind.

Now, one at time, form the same handshapes for each number and simply "flick" the appropriate fingers *twice*. The index finger is flicked for eleven. The index and middle finger are flicked for twelve. Continue to do the same right through fifteen. See, that was easy!

There is a variation in signing sixteen through nineteen. Some people form these number signs by starting with signing the number ten then adding six, seven, eight, or nine.

Moving right along, let's take on numbers sixteen through nineteen, which we'll refer to as the "swing outs." The good news is that the finger positions for numbers that contain six through nine remain constant. These numbers begin with the palm facing you and then "swing out" to face the receiver. Forming the number sixteen begins by touching the thumb to the pinky, palm facing you, then swinging out to face the receiver. The numbers seventeen through nineteen are formed in the same manner, by first touching your thumb to the appropriate fingers then swinging out.

Keep in mind these instructions have been simplified in order to give you a survival guide to signing numbers. When you journey further into your studies of sign language, you will be exposed to a multitude of variations when it comes to signing numbers. Nonetheless, by mastering the basics shown in this chapter, you will have a wonderful head start.

Counting to Ninety

You made it through two whole sets of numbers! You're doing a remarkable job. To reward you for all your hard work, we'll now finish off with the easier numbers.

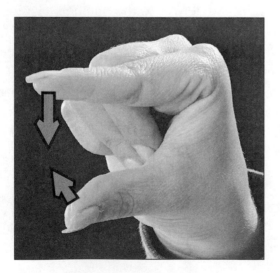

◄ **TWENTY:** The number twenty uses the index finger and the thumb only. Simply bring the index finger and thumb together.

In order to form the handshapes for the numbers thirty, forty, fifty, sixty, seventy, eighty, and ninety, you will need to sign the basic number first, such as three, four, or five. You will then sign a zero. Take a look at the following images.

Counting

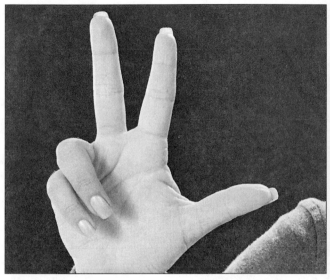

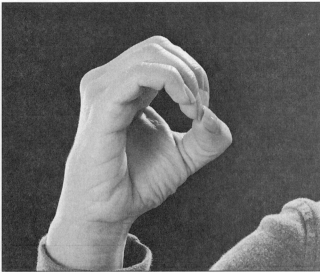

30 ▲**THIRTY:** To sign "thirty," sign the number three, then zero.

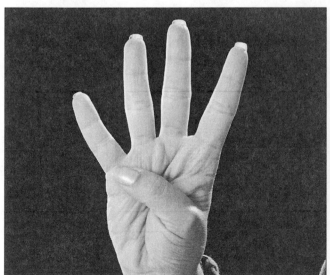

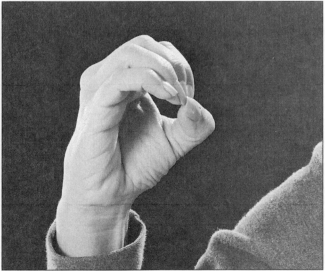

40 ▲**FORTY:** To sign "forty," sign the number four, then zero.

Counting

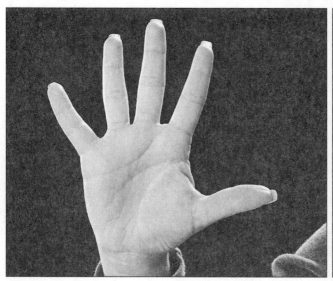

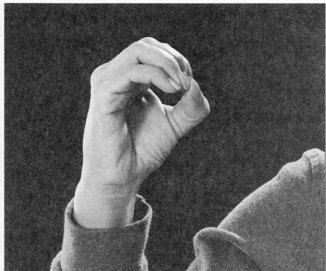

50 ▲ **FIFTY:** To sign "fifty," sign the number five, then zero.

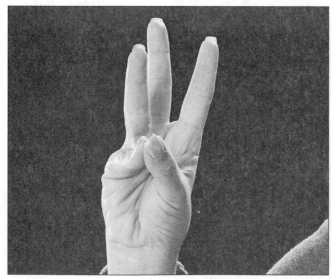

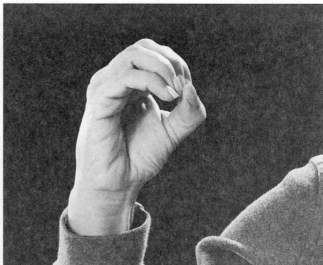

60 ▲ **SIXTY:** To sign "sixty," sign the number six, then zero.

Counting

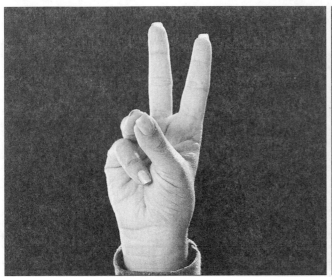 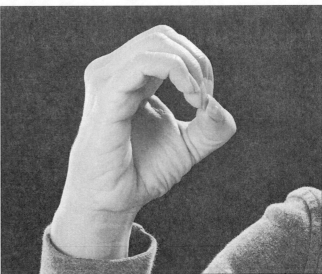

70 ▲ **SEVENTY:** To sign "seventy," sign the number seven, then zero.

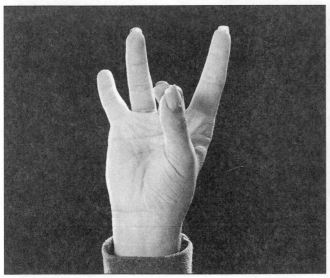 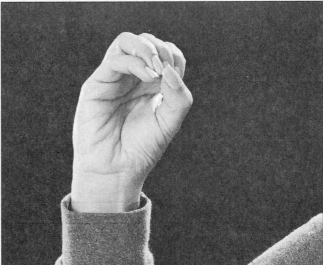

80 ▲ **EIGHTY:** To sign "eighty," sign the number eight, then zero.

Counting

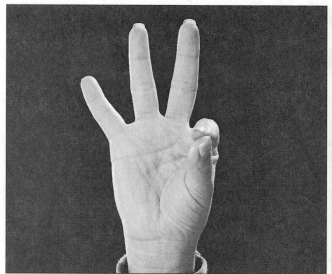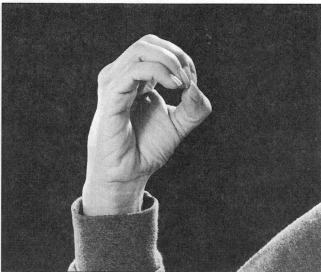

90

▲ **NINETY:** To sign "ninety," sign the number nine, then zero.

If you take your sign language studies further, such as enrolling in a sign language course, you will learn that there are a few shortcuts to numbers. However, for now, all you need is to master the basic numbers.

Big Numbers and Fractions

Sensational! You have made it all the way up to ninety-nine applying Roman numerals. The big numbers—hundreds, thousands, millions—require the simple application of modified Roman numerals. For instance, to sign "one million," sign the number one, then tap the "M" hand twice in the left palm.

Fractions

While the thought of fractions may make you groan, the good news is that they are easy to sign. They are signed exactly the way they appear, one number over the other. They merely use simple numbers.

Counting

 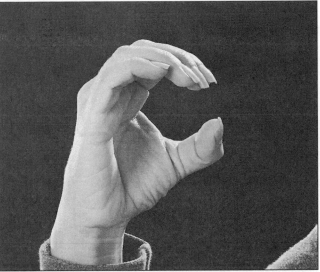

100 ▲ **ONE HUNDRED:** The letter "C" represents the Roman numeral for 100. Sign the number one, then the letter "C." You can continue in this same pattern for 200, 300, and so on.

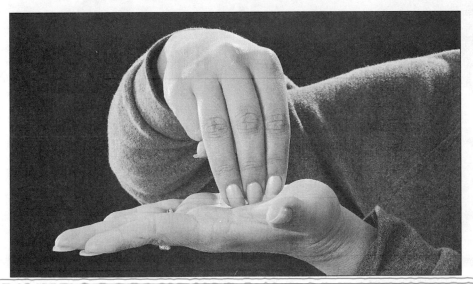

1,000 ▲ **1,000:** The letter "M" is used as the Roman numeral 1,000. Sign the number one, then place the "M" hand on the left "open" palm. You can continue in this same pattern for 2,000, 3,000, and so on.

Fractions

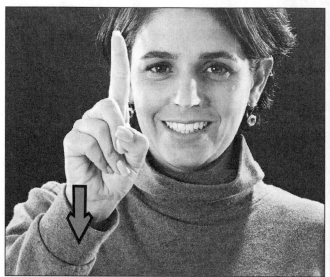

1/2 ▲ **ONE HALF:** To sign "one half," form the handshape for the number one. Then, while moving your hand downward, change the handshape to the number two.

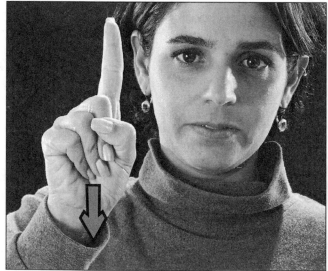

1/4 ▲ **ONE QUARTER:** To sign "one quarter," form the handshape for the number one. Then, while moving your hand downward, change the handshape to the number four.

Fractions

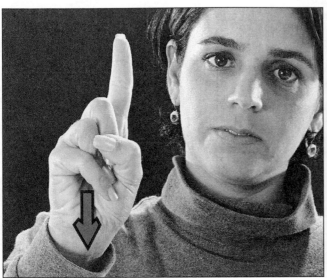

1/3 ▲ **ONE THIRD:** To sign "one third," form the handshape for the number one. Then, while moving your hand downward, change the handshape to the number three.

2/3 ▲ **TWO THIRDS:** To sign "two thirds," form the handshape for the number two. Then, while moving your hand downward, change the handshape to the number three.

Money and Technology

Now you're going to combine your basic numbers with money-related signs. Everyone likes to have money, and the first sign indicates that money is in your hand.

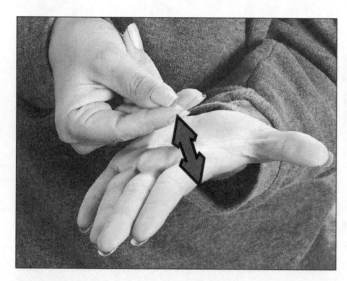

◀ **MONEY:** To sign "money," tap the back of the modified "O" hand on the left "open" palm several times.

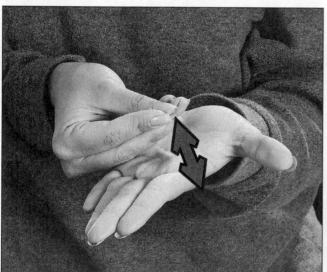

▲ **RICH:** In order to form the sign for "rich," you begin by signing "money," then change to a downward-curved "open five" hand, and pull up. This upward motion represents a stack of money. The higher you raise the stack, the richer you are.

Money

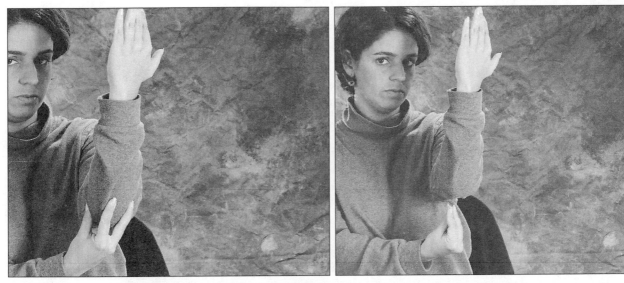

▲ **POOR:** To sign "poor," hold the elbow with the fingertips then draw hand downward to a modified "O," imitating holes in the clothes.

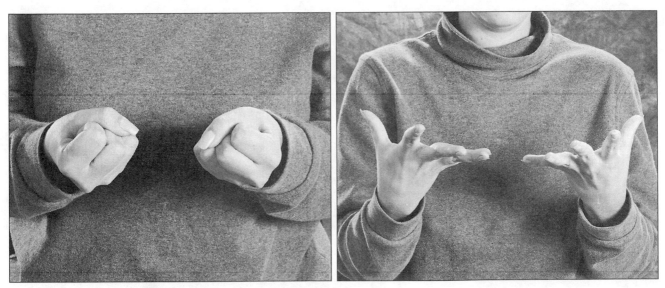

▲ **MANY:** To sign "many," use the "S" hands, closed fists facing up, and open hands quickly many times.

Money

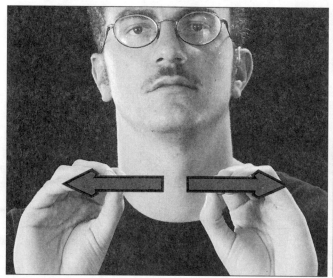

▲ **NONE:** To sign "none," move the "O" hands apart.

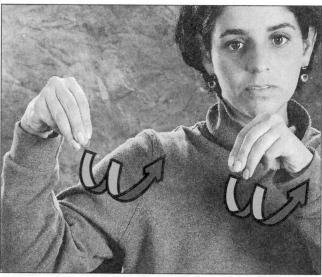

▲ **SELL, SALE, SHOP:** To sign "sell," "sale," or "shop," use the modified "O" hands and move the wrists back and forth.

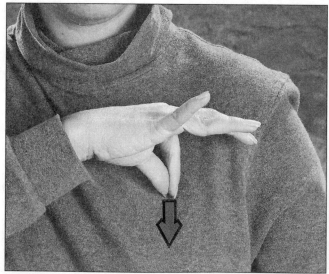

▲ **PROFIT:** To sign "profit," move the "F" hand down over the heart, imitating placing money in a pocket.

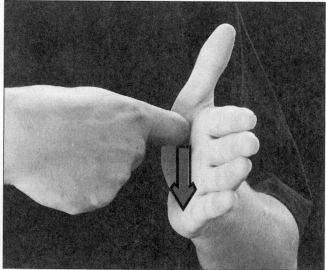

▲ **TAX, COST, PRICE:** To sign "tax," "cost," or "price," draw the "X" hand down the left palm.

Money

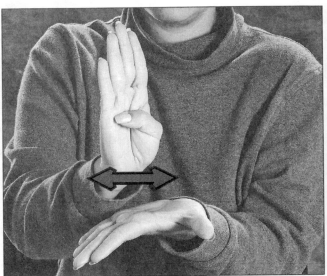

▲ **BUSINESS:** To sign "business," move the "B" hand side to side on the vertical open palm of the left hand several times.

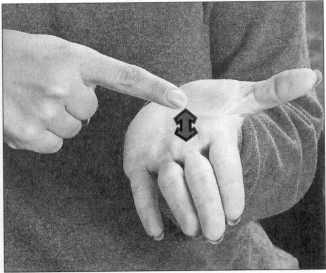

▲ **OWE:** To sign "owe," tap the index finger of the "D" hand on the left "open" palm several times.

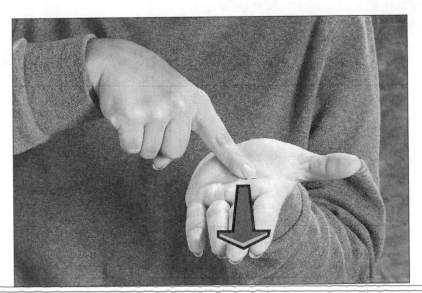

▲ **PAY:** To sign "pay," draw the index finger of the "D" hand across the left "open" palm.

Money

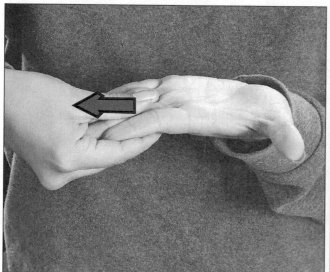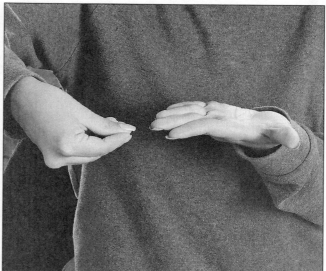

▲ **DOLLAR:** To sign "dollar," grasp the fingers of the left "flat" palm with the right hand and pull away.

Signing Everyday Numbers

Numbers fill our daily lives. To help manage all those numbers, an easy rule to follow is to sign numbers exactly the way they are spoken. When you want to tell someone your phone number, you will sign it one number at a time. Phone numbers are grouped with the area code first, followed by three numbers, then by four numbers. Simply hesitate, just a tad, in between each group of numbers: 555 (hesitate), 555 (hesitate), 5555.

Do not drop your hands; just hesitate.

Often, when discussing money in an ASL conversation, you will see "dollar" signed first, followed by the amount. This may sound strange, but look at how we actually write dollar amounts: $19.00. We always write the dollar sign first, so it's not so strange after all! (Unbelievably, though, the word "bank" is fingerspelled.)

Here is an example of the three different ways you could sign the number 1900.

1. When referring to 1900 as "nineteen hundred," sign "nineteen," followed by the letter "C."
2. When signing 1900 to represent "one thousand nine hundred," sign "one," followed by "M," then "nine," followed by "C."
3. When signing 1900 to represent nineteen dollars (or $19.00), sign "dollar," then "nineteen."

Technology

There are two last signs to learn for this chapter. To keep up with modern-day technology, you need to know how to sign "fax" and "e-mail." There may be regional differences between these technology signs, but here are some of the most common. Signing "fax" is easy; just fingerspell it! The sign for "e-mail" is terrific, as it demonstrates direction. To sign e-mail that is coming in or going out, form an "E" with your right hand, and form a "C" with your left hand. The "E" hand represents the e-mail. The "C" hand represents the computer. Slide your "E" hand through your "C" hand toward you for incoming e-mail, or slide the "E" outward, away from you, for outgoing mail. You might see other ways to sign "e-mail," but to date, this one is the most clear and visual. Ⓔ

Chapter 9

Variety Is the Spice of Life

Conversation is full of description; it's what adds fun to the otherwise mundane. In this chapter, you will learn how to use descriptions to identify someone and to express your emotions and feelings. In addition, we'll throw in dashes of colors just to make it even more exciting.

Describing People

People are very different from one another. Think of how boring the world would be if everyone were the same! Things like hair color, height, and eye color are all characteristics that distinguish an individual. We use these characteristics to describe others. In sign language, there are certain rules to follow for describing people.

Descriptions of people tend to follow a particular order, and gender is always mentioned first. It is then followed by the height, color of the hair and hairstyle, and body type. If the person being described has any distinguishing features, these can then also be described. For example, someone may have a very large smile, beautiful blue eyes, or perhaps a certain mannerism.

The sign for "face" is formed by circling your face with the index finger. The sign for "hair" is formed by touching or stroking your hair. When you want to describe someone's hairstyle, you simply mime the hairstyle. Perhaps you have used mime when describing someone with a mustache or beard. Natural gestures serve as wonderful enhancers to signing. It is perfectly okay to use them. In fact, you are encouraged to use natural gestures, facial expressions, and body language.

In the next few sections, you will learn how to sign colors, clothing, and emotions to help you better describe yourself and others. So take a look in the mirror or at others around you, and get ready to start describing their appearance!

Color My World

Learning to sign colors in groups according to location (that is, where on the body they are signed) is the best way to put them to memory. All the colors that are signed on the face are described here:

- Pink and red are formed on the lips.
- Brown and tan are stroked on the side of the face.
- Orange is squeezed on the cheek.
- Black is formed on the eyebrow.

Colors

▲ **COLORS:** To sign "colors," wiggle the four fingers slightly at the mouth.

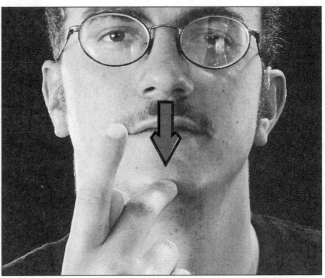

▲ **PINK:** To sign "pink," stroke the lower lip with the tip of the middle finger of the "P" hand.

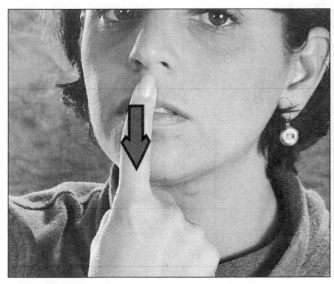

▲ **RED:** To sign "red," stroke the index finger or the "R" hand down the lips.

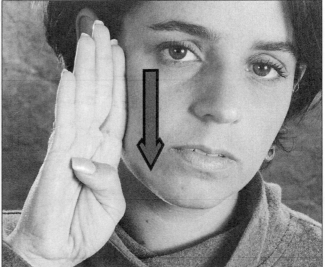

▲ **BROWN:** To sign "brown," draw the "B" hand down the cheek.

Color

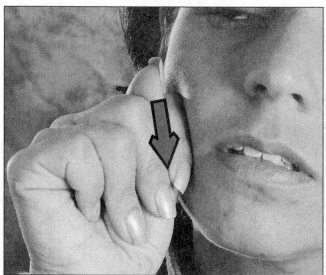

▲ **TAN:** To sign "tan," draw the "T" hand down the cheek.

▲ **ORANGE:** To sign "orange," squeeze the "S" hand near the mouth. This sign can also be formed by squeezing the "S" hand in the cheek area.

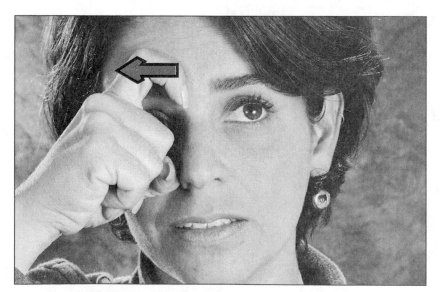

▲ **BLACK:** To sign "black," draw the slightly hooked index finger across the eyebrow.

The next set of colors applies initializing. These colors are formed in the fingerspelling position with the added element of "shaking."

- Blue
- Green
- Purple
- Yellow

FACT

The sign for "orange" can have a different meaning. The hand position near the mouth often implies orange juice, while the hand position on the cheek implies the color.

Color

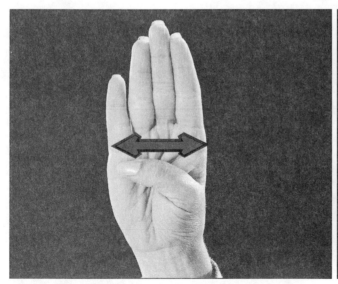
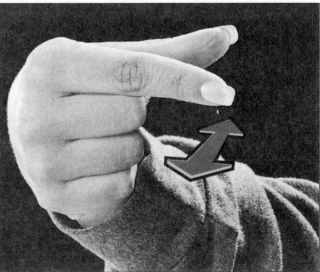

▲ **BLUE:** To sign "blue," shake the "B" hand gently side to side.

▲ **GREEN:** To sign "green," shake the "G" hand gently side to side.

Color

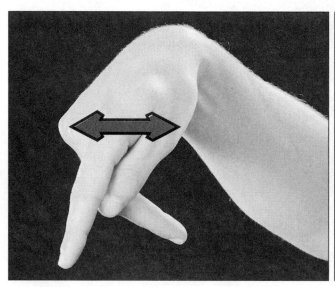

▲**PURPLE:** To sign "purple," shake the "P" hand gently side to side.

▲**YELLOW:** To sign "yellow," shake the "Y" hand gently side to side.

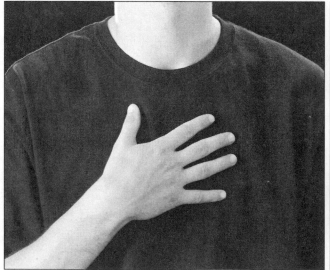

▲**WHITE:** To sign "white," draw the "open five" hand forward from the chest into an "O" hand.

Dress Me Up

Your visualization and mime skills will be put to the test in this section as you learn how to describe apparel. We'll start with the easy stuff. To sign "shirt," all you need to do is tug on your shirt. See how simple that is! You can describe the sleeve lengths of shirts with visualization. Just extend your left arm and tap at the appropriate length with the side of the "B" hand: Tap the wrist for long sleeves, the forearm for three-quarter length sleeves, and the upper arm for short sleeves. Generally, you can point to any item of clothing in order to describe it.

Next, visualize a spaghetti strap top. Now mime sign pulling up the straps. (You know, the kind of top whose straps constantly are sliding off the shoulders.) Still stimulating your visualization and mime skills, let's picture putting on a pair of pants. In order for you to put them on, you need to pull them up. Okay, so guess how you sign pants. If you answered pulling them up to the waist, you are correct! Of course, an outfit wouldn't be complete without a pair of shoes.

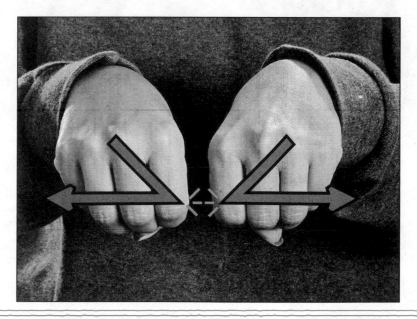

▲ **SHOES:** To sign "shoes," visualize Dorothy in *The Wizard of Oz* clicking her heels, and tap the "S" hands together twice.

What We Look Like

They say that beauty is in the eye of the beholder. The sign for "beautiful" can be communicated more strongly using the eyes and facial expressions. This is especially true if you are trying to describe someone who is a knockout. You have seen, many times, the natural facial expression that enhances the sign for "beautiful." Try to envision that specific facial expression, the one where the man meets the woman or vice versa, and one or the other is smitten. You have seen many examples of this type of facial expression on television commercials, in stage performances, and in real life. For instance, you may notice stars in the eyes, rapid blinking, a dazed or dazzled look in the eye, and often a certain tilt to the head.

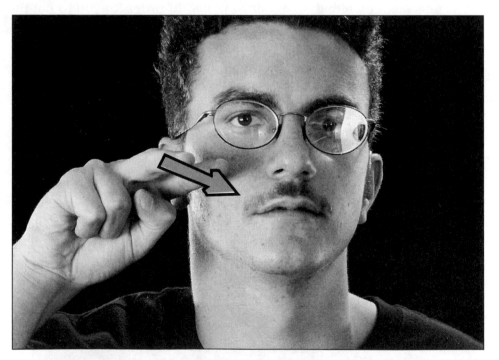

▲ **LOOK, SEE:** To sign "look" or "see," move the "V" hand forward away from the eye. This sign may be executed with one or both hands and can be moved in the direction of the person or object being "looked" at.

Facial Expressions

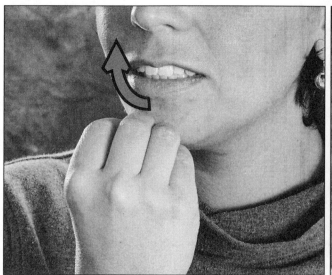

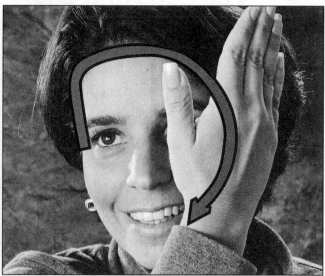

▲ **BEAUTIFUL:** To sign "beautiful," use a closed hand starting at the chin, open to a "flat" hand while circling the face.

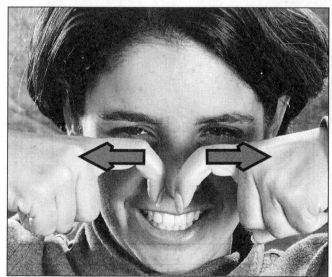

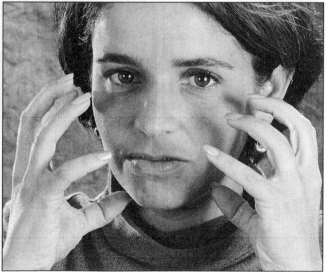

▲ **UGLY:** To sign "ugly," separate the "X" hands. To modify this sign, use one "X" hand drawn across the nose and mouth, rather than two. This image demonstrates the sign with severity.

▲ **CHUBBY:** To sign "chubby," place a "curved five" hand on either side of the cheeks of your face.

The Good and Bad

Now let's take a look at how we use sign language to describe our emotions and feelings. As you begin learning the following signs, don't forget to add appropriate facial expressions. The stronger the feeling, whether it is positive or negative, the stronger the facial expression.

Emotions and Feelings

▲ **HAPPY:** To sign "happy," use a modified "B" hand. Pat your chest upward several times and smile.

▲ **GROUCHY:** To sign "grouchy," bend and unbend the "curved five" hands several times in front of the face.

Emotions and Feelings

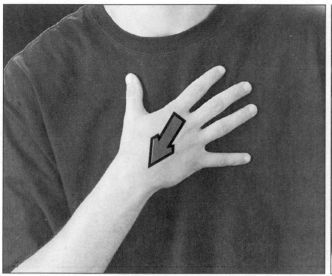

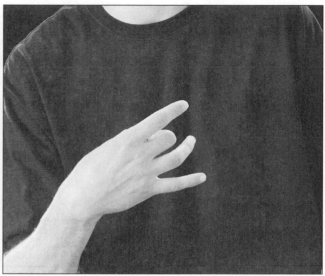

▲**LIKE:** To sign "like," place the open "five" hand on the chest and pull hand away while touching the thumb to the middle finger.

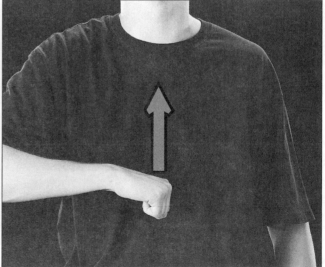

▲**CRAZY:** To sign "crazy," pivot the "curved five" hand several times at the side of the head.

▲**PROUD:** To sign "proud," draw the "A" hand straight up the chest, and straighten your back.

Emotions and Feelings

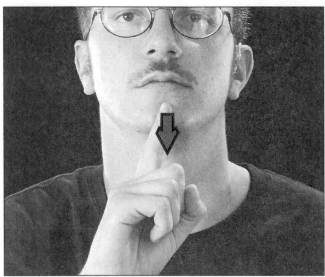

▲ **LONELY:** To sign "lonely," draw the index finger of the "D" hand down the chin.

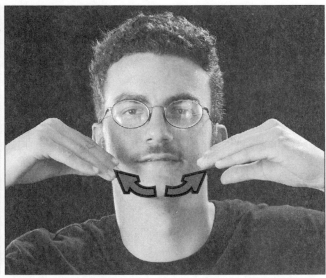

▲ **SMILE, FRIENDLY:** To sign "smile" or "friendly," draw both modified "B" hands up and away from the mouth, imitating a "smiley face."

▲ **TIRED:** To sign "tired," drop bent hands slightly at center of chest and lean forward.

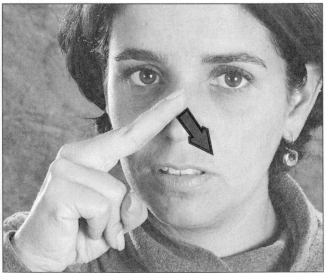

▲ **FUNNY:** To sign "funny," brush the index finger or the index and middle fingers off the tip of the nose.

Emotions and Feelings

▲ **JEALOUS:** To sign "jealous," twist the pinky at the mouth.

▲ **HEART:** To sign "heart," use both index fingers to trace an outline of a heart shape on the chest.

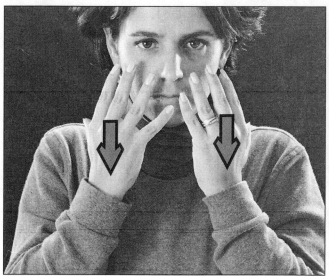

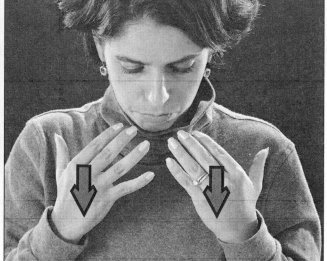

▲ **SAD, DEPRESSED, CRY:** To sign "sad," "depressed," or "cry," drop "open five" hands down from the face, while dropping head and looking sad.

Pronouns and Possessives

If you have the opportunity to go to a social event in the Deaf community, you will see a room come alive with signs, natural gestures, facial expressions, and body language. The Deaf are fabulous storytellers and easily capture your attention with the full animation that rounds out their storytelling. Depending on your interest and the application of your ASL skills, someday you may find yourself signing a story. However, in order to build that skill, you will need to learn possessives and a few pronouns.

Pronouns

▲ **I, ME:** To sign "I" or "me," use the index finger of the "D" hand and point to yourself.

▲ **YOU:** To sign "you," point the index finger of the "D" hand outward.

Pronouns

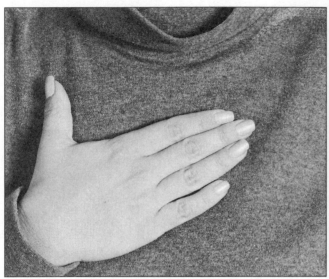

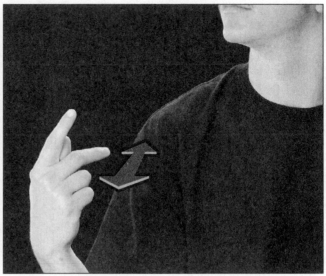

▲ **MY, MINE:** To sign "my" or "mine," place the "flat" hand on the chest.

▲ **US, WE:** To sign "us" or "we," move the "K" hand back and forth.

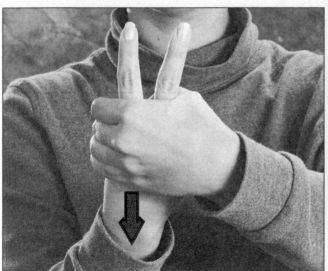

▲ **BOTH:** To sign "both," pull the index and middle fingers through the left "C" hand.

Possessives

The following illustration demonstrates the basic root sign for "your, yours, his, hers, theirs." To sign all of these words, all we have to do is make only a few slight changes to the basic form. To begin, we will sign just the root by moving the "flat" hand forward slightly. Good! Try that once again.

Let us suppose that you are in a shopping mall, and you have just seen someone wearing a nice pair of shoes that you like. The sign vocabulary in this chapter will enable you to express just that thought.

Now you are ready to sign "his, hers." To indicate "his," you will need to sign "male" first, followed by "your." To indicate "hers," sign "female" first, followed by "your." The signs for "his" and "hers" are compound signs, in other words, that use two or more signs to convey an idea. The sign for "theirs" is formed by moving the hand slightly left to right to indicate more than one person.

Possessives

▲ **ROOT SIGN OF YOUR, YOURS, HIS, HERS, THEIRS**

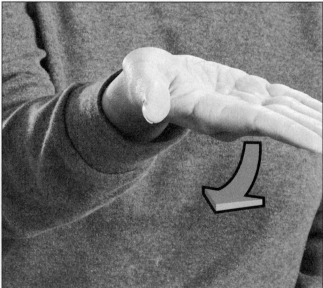

▲ **THESE, THOSE:** To sign "these" or "those," move the "flat" hand, palm up, forward and to the right slightly.

Chapter 10

Friends, Family, and Acquaintances

Now that you know some signs to help you describe people, we're going to take it a step further and add genders and relationships. Once you are finished with this chapter, you will be able to identify specific members of your family, such as an aunt or brother, and also have the tools to be able to begin signing their occupations.

Genders

The sign vocabulary that you are acquiring is becoming larger with each chapter. In previous chapters, you may have noticed that some of the signs were repeated, but the repetition featured a slight variation that changed the meaning of the sign. Most of the changes in these images are subtle and are described in the text or shown with the arrows. Some of the signs were the same, but they had two different meanings depending on the context of the sentence. In this book, we show you repetition in order to include the sign in new groups of signs with new meanings. In some instances, this is to show you that one of the best tools a signer can have is a large batch of synonyms. They are wonderful tools!

The sign for "male" can also be "man," "gentleman," "guy," or "boy." The sign for "female" can also mean "woman," "lady," or "girl." You could be in a store and say, "Excuse me, Miss" to the clerk. This expression would still be signed using the sign for "female."

Genders

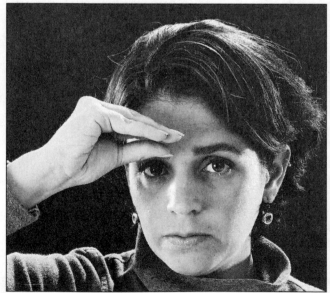 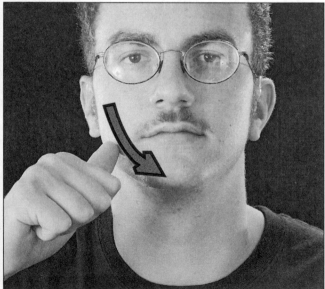

▲ **MALE:** To sign "male," move the flattened "O" hand slightly away from the forehead, imitating tipping the brim of a hat.

▲ **FEMALE:** To sign "female," stroke the "A" hand down the cheek to the chin, imitating the string of a bonnet.

Children

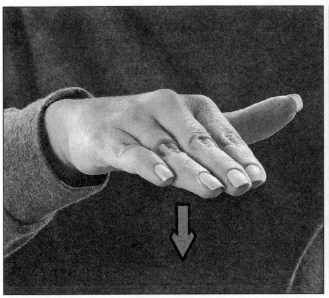

▲ **CHILD:** The sign for "child" can indicate various ages. Just extend your arm, and raise it to the age appropriate height. If you want to sign "children," all you need to do is pat the head of several imaginary "children" all around you.

▲ **BABY:** To sign "baby," imitate rocking a baby.

Family Relationships

You've learned the signs that represent the core of a family: male, female, and child. Next, you'll learn how to be more specific with gender signs. In general, the following signs for family demonstrate a gender sign first, followed by a second sign that is appropriate to the meaning. Once again, these are a series of two or more signs that create a compound sign. In reality, this makes it easy for the signer to remember how to form the sign.

Family Relationships

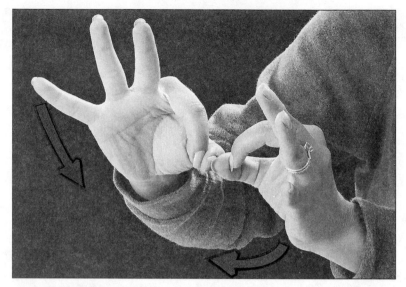

▲ **FAMILY:** To sign "family," circle the "F" hands forward until the pinkies touch.

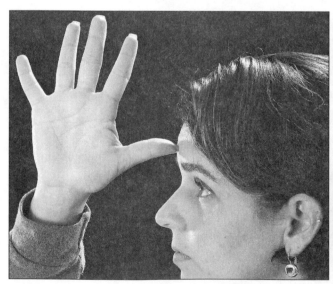

▲ **FATHER:** To sign "father," tap the thumb of the "open five" hand on the forehead.

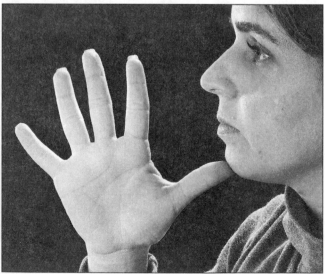

▲ **MOTHER:** To sign "mother," tap the thumb of the "open five" hand on the chin.

Family Relationships

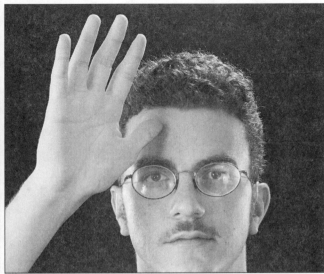

▲ **PARENTS:** To sign "parents," first sign "mother" and then immediately sign "father." These two signs create the compound sign for "parents."

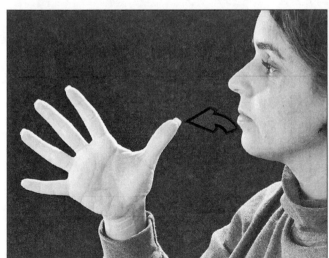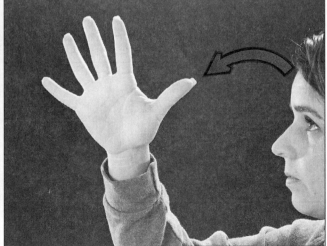

▲ **GRANDMOTHER:** To sign "grandmother," sign "mother" then move forward with an arched movement off the chin, indicating generations.

▲ **GRANDFATHER:** To sign "grandfather," sign "father" then move forward with an arched movement off the forehead, indicating generations.

Family Relationships

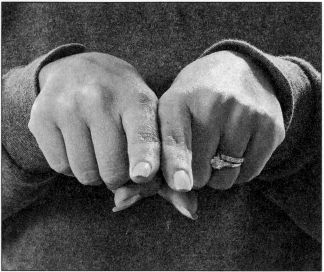

▲ **MARRIAGE:** You make the sign for "marriage" by tightly sealing the hands together, representing a bond.

▲ **SAME:** The sign for "same" can be formed with two different variations. The first variation is shown in the image. The second variation is to sign "male" or "female," then place the right "D" hand on top of the left "D" hand.

ESSENTIAL

To sign another variation of "parents," tap the "P" hand above and below the cheekbone. Using the "P" hand to sign "parents" is an example of an initialized sign. In fact, if you use the "A" hand in place of the "P" hand, you are now signing the word "adults."

The signs for "husband" and "wife" are compound signs. To form these signs, you will need to sign the gender first, then the sign for "marriage." In other words, sign "female" and "marriage" for "wife." Sign "male" and "marriage" for "husband."

The signs for "brother" and "sister" are also compound signs. To form these signs, you will need to sign the gender first, then the sign for "same." In other words, sign "male" and "same" for "brother." Sign "female" and "same" for "sister."

By this time, you should have mastered the location of the female and male signs. Having mastered genders, you can easily sign the remaining family members. These signs are initialized and gently tapped in the appropriate gender location:

- Uncle: Tap the "U" hand at the temple.
- Nephew: Tap the "N" hand at the temple.
- Niece: Tap the "N" hand at the chin.
- Aunt: Tap the "A" hand at the chin.

People We Know

In this section, you will learn to affix the "person" sign to create compound signs used to describe people. (Of course, the "person" sign can also be used alone to simply mean "person.") Learning to affix or apply the "person" sign gives you a powerful tool for communication. When the "person" sign is used as an ending, it can be referred to in sign language dictionaries as any of the following: "person," "agent," or the "er" sign. In this book, we will refer to it as "the 'person' sign."

When the "person" sign is applied to a sign, it is now considered a compound sign. When used as a compound sign, it adds clarity. This compound sign identifies whether we are talking about an item or a person. For example, you can imitate playing the piano, and this is clearly understood when signed. However, if you want to sign "pianist," you would sign "piano" then add the "person" sign. Another example is to sign "dance" then add the "person" sign to signify that you mean "dancer." In Chapter 11, where we learn to sign about sports, you will have many opportunities to apply the "person" sign. With one sign, you can change a sport into the player of that sport.

However, not all signs affix or use the "person" sign to refer to occupations or sports. You will also learn some signs that do not require affixing the "person" sign.

People We Know

▲ **PERSON:** To sign "person," use both "flat" hands, palms facing each other, and move hands straight down.

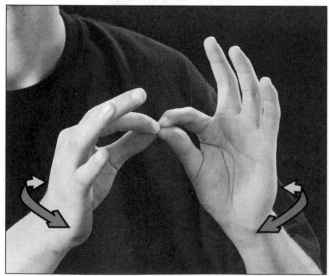

▲ **INTERPRETER:** To sign "interpreter," twist "F" hands alternately back and forth several times, then add "person."

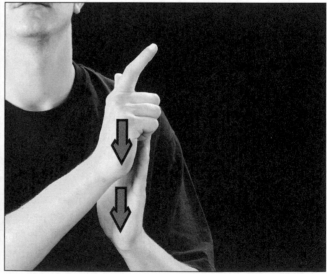

▲ **LAWYER:** To sign "lawyer," tap the "L" hand to the top and bottom of the left vertical hand, then add "person."

People We Know

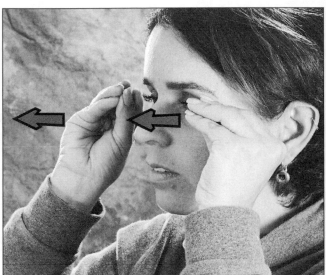

▲ **TEACHER:** To sign "teacher," move the flattened "O" hands forward from the temples, then add "person."

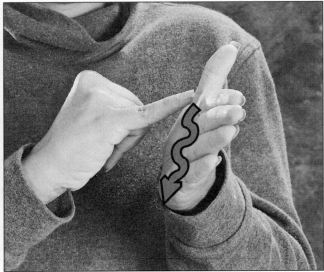

▲ **ARTIST:** To sign "artist," draw the "I" hand in a wavy movement down the left "open" palm, then add "person."

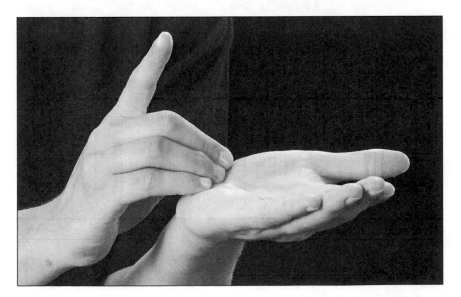

▲ **DOCTOR:** To sign "doctor," place the "D" hand on the inside of your wrist, imitating taking a pulse.

People We Know

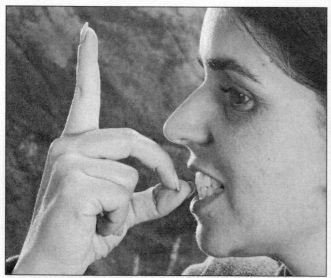

▲ **DENTIST:** To sign "dentist," tap the teeth with the "D" hand.

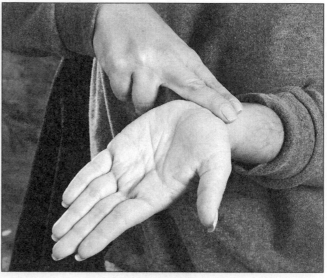

▲ **NURSE:** To sign "nurse," tap the "N" hand on the wrist, imitating taking a pulse.

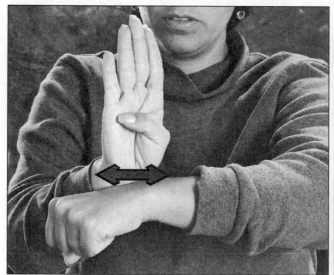

▲ **BUSINESSMAN, BUSINESSWOMAN:** To sign "businessman" or "businesswoman," move the "B" hand side to side on top of the "S" hand, then sign "man" or "woman."

▲ **POLICE OFFICER:** To sign "police officer," tap the "C" hand over the heart, representing the officer's badge.

The Workplace

The Americans with Disabilities Act, or ADA, has the potential to affect almost any workplace. Keep this in mind when applying for a new job. The knowledge of sign language on your resume certainly could give you a better chance to secure a position you may be seeking.

◀ **WORK:** To sign "work," strike the "S" hands twice.

Many businesses can be affected by the ADA's rules and regulations. Today, when employers want to hire new employees, they benefit by hiring those who have awareness and sensitivity toward those people who are protected by the ADA. There is a chance that you may not realize how far-reaching the ADA can be. "Public accommodations" is a broad term, and there is a very good chance that public accommodations, as mandated by the ADA, may be enforced where you are currently employed. Here are a few examples of workplaces that the ADA could affect:

- Movie theaters, concert halls, stadiums, auditoriums, convention centers, lecture halls, museums, and libraries.
- Sales and rental establishments, bakeries, grocery stores, hardware stores, shopping centers, health spas, gymnasiums, golf courses, and bowling alleys.

- Service establishments; hospitals; professional offices of healthcare providers, accountants, lawyers, or insurance agents; pharmacies; funeral parlors; travel services; beauty and barber shops; and banks.
- Public transportation, terminals, depots, and airlines.
- Elementary, secondary, undergraduate, postgraduate, private and public schools, and other places of education; nurseries; day care centers; social services centers; and law enforcement agencies.

The ADA affects virtually everything that police officers and law enforcement agencies do, such as arresting, booking, and holding suspects, interrogating witnesses, and operating emergency call centers.

FACT

Whether a workplace is affected by the rules and regulations mandated by the ADA depends on the size of the place, business, or service. Though this is true, the point is that you may still benefit by learning and taking a sign language course. At the same time, you would also be preparing yourself to help others who may need equal access to communication.

In addition, the ADA requires law enforcement agencies to make reasonable modifications. An example of this would be modifying their regular practice of handcuffing arrestees behind their backs. Instead, the arresting officer will handcuff deaf individuals in front in order for the person to sign or write notes. Sometimes they will even be unhandcuffed during the hearing if they need to answer a question. Ⓔ

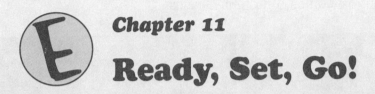

Chapter 11

Ready, Set, Go!

It's time to play! In this chapter, you will learn how to apply a simple classifier to show physical movements, such as walking, sitting, and dancing. You will also be introduced to sports signs and learn how to transform them into compound signs. Remember, it's playtime, so have fun while you learn the subjects in this chapter.

Let Your Fingers Do the Walking

A signer can show many movements by simply moving the index and middle fingers into various positions. This handshape is called a "classifier," and the hand position is an "inverted V." This classifier is used to demonstrate movements or body positions. We'll start off with two of the most common movement signs.

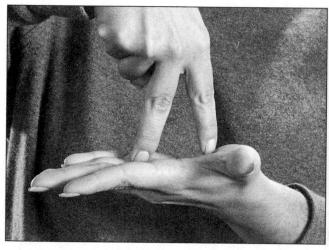

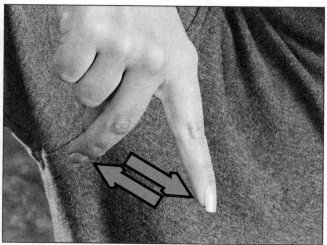

▲ **STAND:** To sign "stand," use the index and middle fingers to make an "inverted V." Place it onto the left "open" palm, imitating a pair of legs standing.

▲ **WALK:** To sign "walk," make an "inverted V" and alternately swing the index and middle fingers, imitating walking.

FACT

This application of classifiers when used by nurses, physical therapists, and medical professionals is extremely helpful in demonstrating to a patient how he or she needs to be positioned.

Classifier Hand Puppet

Here is a cute idea for early childhood providers or anyone who has or knows children. We are going to learn to make and apply a modified hand puppet using a classifier handshape.

First, make the "inverted V" handshape. Look at it closely. The fingers are the legs, and the back of the hand can be the body. Now, here is where you can use your imagination, with the help of some small doll clothes you can fashion yourself. Let's dress it up! Slip your hand puppet into something comfortable, like a pair of shorts or a skirt. Draw a pair of shoes on your fingertips, or you can put on a pair of socks. (You can create a pair of socks or shoes by recycling the fingertips of an old pair of gloves.) Next, draw on the back of your hand a smiling face with some hair and a shirt. Voilà! You have created a hand puppet, and young children will giggle with delight.

Young children will simply adore the classifier hand puppet. (And you get to have some fun, too!) Let the children dress up their own hand puppet, and watch their imaginations soar.

Your classifier hand is all dressed up, so it's time to kick up your heels and dance. To accomplish this, put your hands back into the "stand" position. The left palm makes a little dance floor for your legs. Are you ready to step out on to the dance floor? Put your right foot in, put your right foot out, put your right foot in, and you shake it all about—by now, you have the idea. When you are tired from shaking it all about, find a chair and sit yourself down. Keep the same hand position and dangle your feet over the edge of the imaginary chair.

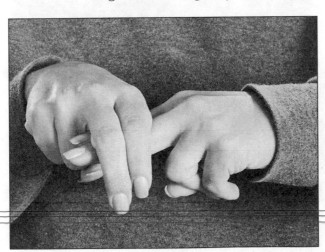

◀ **SIT, CHAIR:** To sign "sit," place the right "N" fingers over the extended left "N" fingers, imitating legs dangling.

Sport Signs

In this section, you will apply the "person" ending that we introduced in Chapter 10. This is a great chance to practice your newfound knowledge. The next set of vocabulary words will be related to sports. However, you can double that vocabulary set by simply signing the sport and then transforming it to indicate the player. For instance, if you sign the word "golf" then add the "person" sign, the sign becomes "golfer."

The following images of sport signs serve a dual purpose. From them, you will learn to sign specific sports, while at the same time you will learn how to form a compound sign. As mentioned before, the compound sign is made by simply adding the "person" sign immediately after signing any one of these sports signs described. Just to refresh your memory, let's take a look at the "person" sign.

▲ **PERSON:** To sign "person," use both "flat" hands, palms facing each other, and move hands straight down.

Sports Signs

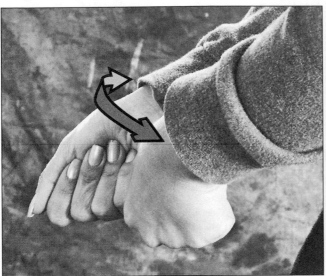

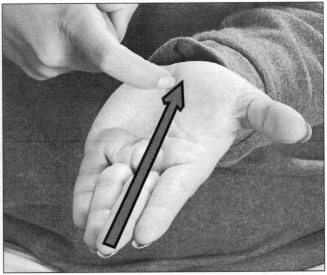

▲ **GOLF:** To sign "golf," hold both fists as though they are imitating swinging a golf club. Add the "person" sign and now the sign becomes "golfer."

▲ **HOCKEY:** To sign "hockey," use the bent index finger to sweep across the "open" left palm, imitating a hockey stick. Add the "person" sign, and the sign becomes "hockey player."

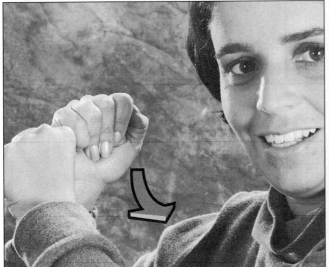

▲ **BASEBALL:** To sign "baseball," hold both fists at shoulder level, imitating holding a baseball bat. Add the "person" sign, and the sign becomes "baseball player."

▲ **SWIMMING:** To sign "swimming," move both arms, imitating a swimming stroke. Add the "person" sign, and the sign becomes "swimmer."

Sports Signs

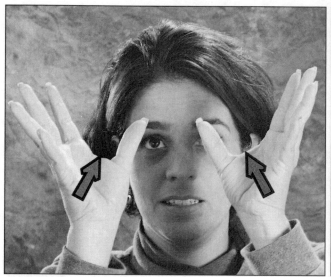

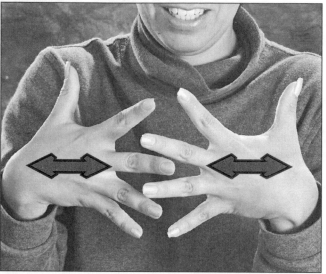

▲ BASKETBALL: To sign "basketball," hold an imaginary basketball and imitate the action of shooting a basket. Add the "person" sign, and now the sign becomes "basketball player."

▲ FOOTBALL: To sign "football," use both "open five" hands, palms facing the body, and bring fingers together several times, imitating two teams crashing together. Add the "person" sign, and now the sign becomes "football player."

FACT

The football huddle was invented by Paul D. Hubbard. Hubbard was a quarterback on the Gallaudet football team, and his opponents were deaf. The team learned that the opposing teams were reading their signed messages and could understand their team plays. Therefore, Hubbard decided to make a team huddle. This huddle is now used by all football teams.

Additional Compound Signs

By now, you have begun to realize how you can transform the different sports signs to mean the players themselves by forming a compound sign. However, sports signs aren't the only ones you can use in compound signs. There are many compound signs in sign language. As your acquisition of sign vocabulary grows, you will begin to recognize many of these types of compound signs. You will also realize how easy it is to form a compound sign, which adds detail and clarity to the topic. Here are two more examples of using compound signs.

Compound Signs

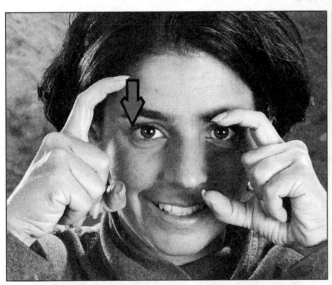

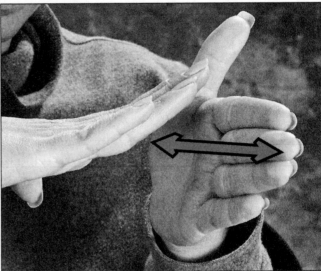

▲ CAMERA: To sign "camera," hold an imaginary camera up to the eye and press the shutter button with the index finger. Remember, adding the "person" sign changes this sign to "photographer."

▲ PAINT: To sign "paint," brush the right fingertips back and forth across the left "open" palm, imitating brush strokes. Add the "person" sign, and now the sign becomes "painter."

Play Ball!

A sports chapter in a sign language book would not be complete without a story about a famous deaf ballplayer. William Ellsworth "Dummy" Hoy was born in 1862. He lived to be nearly 100 years old before passing away in 1961. Hoy was the first deaf professional baseball player in the major leagues.

There are several stories surrounding Hoy and his contributions to the game of baseball. Some of these have been validated by old newspaper clippings from as far back as 1888. In the early days of baseball, all umpire calls were shouted. It is said Hoy was responsible for the creation of the signals for "strike," "safe," and "out." Hoy created these signals because neither he nor the crowd could hear the calls by the home plate umpires. Today these signals are tradition and are used by umpires worldwide.

Some say that the intricate system of hand signals used in baseball and softball games today can be traced back to Hoy. These additional signals would include the manager's call signals to the batter, as well as the outfielders' calls.

William Hoy was one of the few players to have played in four of the five recognized major leagues, and he held an outstanding baseball career record. The crowds loved Hoy and to show their approval, they stood in the bleachers and waved their hats and arms to demonstrate their enthusiasm. Some say this is the first early form of "deaf applause," a visual form of applauding.

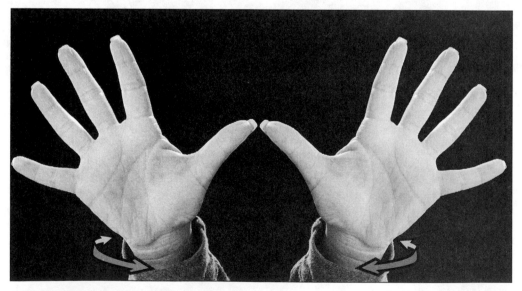

▲ **APPLAUSE:** To sign "applause," you raise both hands high in the air, in an "open five" position, and shake them.

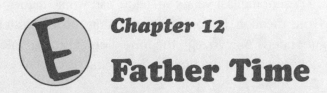

Chapter 12

Father Time

The subject of time is part of our every-day conversations. This chapter will introduce you to many of the common "time" signs. You will quickly learn the months of the year and their fingerspelled abbreviations. There will also be seasons and holiday signs to add to your new sign vocabulary.

Past, Present, and Future

There are a few easy-to-follow rules to use when signing units of time. These rules have been created to add clarity to a signed conversation. One of these rules governs when a signer should apply a "time" sign. The rule is simple: Always sign the time element first when relating a story or an event. For example, if you were describing last year's vacation you would sign "past year" first, then describe your vacation. In conversations using "now," "yesterday," and "tomorrow," the signer needs only to sign the time element once unless there is a change in the conversation of the time period being discussed.

As you can see from the images, signs relating to the future are clearly indicated with a forward-moving arrow. The further you move your arm and hand forward, the further the date is in the future. In reverse, the same applies to signs relating to the past.

Now, try to imagine a physical timeline that goes straight through your body, extending out in front and back behind you. This imaginary line in front and back of you is there to represent the future and the past. All signs indicating the future are made in a forward movement and are out ahead of your body. All signs indicating the past are made with a backward movement and are often pushed behind your shoulder. So, the rule is: The future moves forward, and the past moves backward.

▲ **FUTURE:** To sign "future," use the "flat" hand, move it forward and down.

Past, Present, and Future

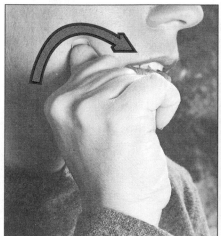

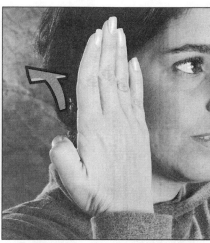

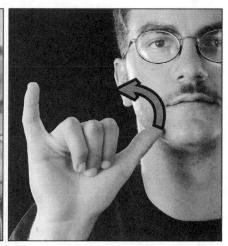

▲ **TOMORROW:** To sign "tomorrow," use the "A" hand on the cheek, and turn it forward and down.

▲ **PAST:** To sign "past," use the "flat" hand, palm facing back, and push it over the shoulder.

▲ **YESTERDAY:** To sign "yesterday," use the "Y" or modified "A" hand on the cheek, and pull it backwards.

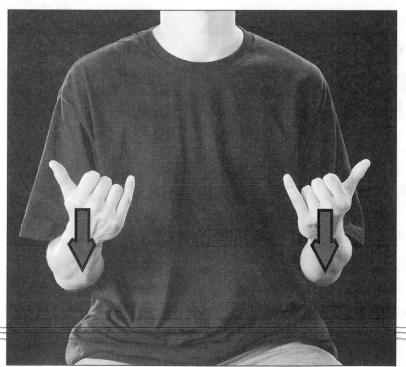

◄ **NOW, PRESENT:** In the timeline, your body is the very center, indicating that you are standing in the "present/now" time. The sign used to indicate the "present" is formed just in front and alongside of your body. The "now" or "present" sign has two variations. It can be made using the bent "flat" hands coming down in front and alongside the body, or the same motion can be made with the "Y" hand, as shown.

Signing a Specific Time

Another way of indicating time is to simply point to your watch. When indicating a specific time, point to the watch, sign the correct number for the time, and then point again to the watch. To the receiver/reader it would look like this: time, number, time. In Chapter 8, you learned how to form the signs for numbers. When indicating time on a clock or watch, you will need to combine "number" signs. It is important to make sure that you learn and remember all of the basic signs for time, as they are used frequently in a signed conversation.

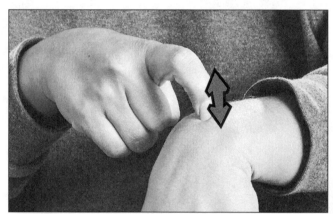

◀ **TIME:** To sign "time," tap the top of the wrist twice, imitating tapping a watch.

▲ **MINUTE:** To sign "minute," place the "D" hand on the left "open" palm, in a vertical position. Move the index finger forward, imitating the hands on a clock.

▲ **HOUR:** To sign "hour," place the "D" hand on the left "open" palm, in a vertical position, then rotate the index finger forward one turn, imitating one hour on the face of a clock.

General Times

Time signs play an important role in conversation. They serve to clarify when an event happened or when it will occur. These signs also assist in indicating verb tenses, when needed. Moving on within the time elements, the next three signs—morning, noon, and night— are iconic in their compositions. Two of these signs were demonstrated in an early chapter. However, we need to take a closer look at these signs now that you have progressed up through the chapters.

The position of the arms for these signs relates closely to the sun's movements as it rises and sets. When holding your left arm stationary in front of you, imagine your arm to be the horizon. The sun comes peeking over the horizon in the morning. At noon, the sun shines down from directly overhead, and at night, the sun disappears again down below the horizon.

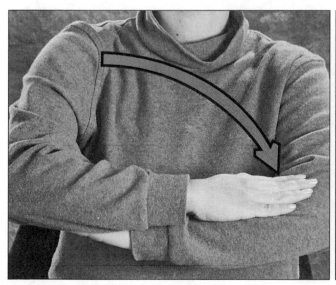

▲ **DAY:** To sign "day," hold the right arm in a vertical position, with the elbow resting on the fingertips of the left arm. Bring the right arm slowly down to rest on the left arm. This sign can be made with the "flat" hand or the "D" hand.

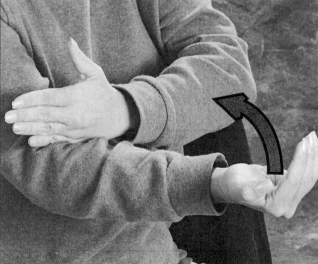

▲ **MORNING:** To sign "morning," hold the stationary left arm across the front of the body and move the right arm up slightly, imitating the sun rising.

General Times

▲ **NOON:** To sign "noon," hold the right arm in a vertical position, with the elbow resting on the fingertips of the left horizontal stationary left arm.

▲ **NIGHT, EVENING:** To sign "night" or "evening," hold the stationary left arm across the front of the body. Move the right hand and arm over the left hand, imitating the sun going down.

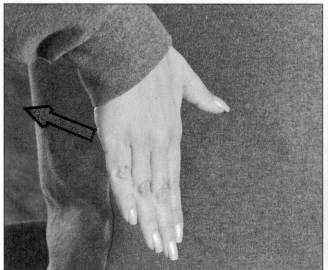

▲ **LATE, NOT YET:** To sign "late" or "not yet," place the "flat" hand near the waist, palm facing back, and push back.

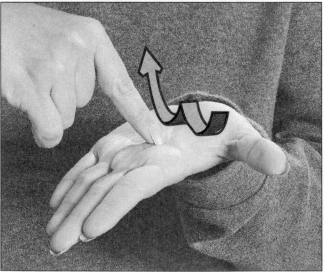

▲ **ONCE IN A WHILE, SOMETIMES:** To sign "once in a while" or "sometimes," swipe the index finger of the "D" hand on the left "open" palm twice.

General Times

▲ **YEAR:** To sign "year," circle the right "S" hand forward and around the left "S" hand, and rest on the top of the left hand.

▲ **NEVER:** To sign "never," move the "flat" hand, palm down, as shown in the image.

Learning the Calendar

Using the alphabet, fingerspell the months of the year. Each month has an abbreviation. The abbreviated form is the preferred way when used in a signed conversation. Your signing skills will be strengthened when you see these abbreviations as a whole word. Seeing an abbreviated sign as a whole sign means you aren't looking to read each letter, but rather that you are seeing the shape of the whole sign. This skill is an important part of beginning to recognize "initialized" and "loan" signs. It is a skill that takes time to master and that will require patience on your part. Here are a few practice tips. Look at the shape that the abbreviation creates rather than the individual letters. Remember to do your hand warmups before you fingerspell.

Abbreviation	Word
J-A-N	January
F-E-B	February
M-A-R	March
A-P-R	April
M-A-Y	May
J-U-N	June
J-U-L	July
A-U-G	August
S-E-P-T	September
O-C-T	October
N-O-V	November
D-E-C	December

The next thing you need to learn is the days of the week. Once again, we borrow from the alphabet and "initialize" nearly all the days of the week. There are three well-known variations in making the signs for the days of the week. These variations, which are only in the movement, are the result of regional and geographical differences. Here are the different ways these signs are made:

- **First variation:** The palm is facing you and the arm moves in a small circle, as if swinging a lasso.
- **Second variation:** The palm is facing you and the arm moves in a small circle, counterclockwise.
- **Third variation:** The palm faces the reader/receiver and moves in a clockwise motion.

These three variations are used throughout the country, and it is best that you are familiar with all three. However, following the rules of fingerspelling, which says the palm must face the reader/receiver, the following chart gives you instructions for the third variation.

Day	Sign direction
Monday	Use the "M" hand, and rotate in a small clockwise circle.
Tuesday	Use the "T" hand, and rotate in a small clockwise circle.
Wednesday	Use the "W" hand, and rotate in a small clockwise circle.
Thursday	Use the "H" hand, and rotate in a small clockwise circle.
Friday	Use the "F" hand, and rotate in a small clockwise circle.
Saturday	Use the "S" hand, and rotate in a small clockwise circle.
Sunday	Signing "Sunday" is a little different. To do this, use the "open five" hands, palms facing out, move in opposite circular motions.

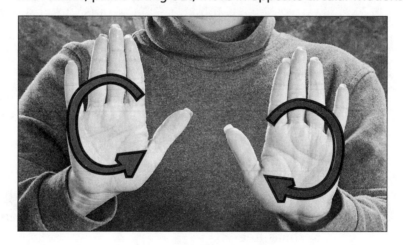

It is easy to remember how to sign the days of the week because you are simply "initializing" the first letter. There are only two small exceptions. Thursday uses the letter "H" because we have already used "T" for Tuesday, and Sunday is not an initialized sign at all. Instead, the sign represents a "wonderful" day.

ALERT!

A signer needs to respect the variations in signs. This is especially true when seeing and using any of the "time" signs. There are thirteen different ways to sign Sunday; three for Monday, Tuesday, Wednesday, and Friday; four for Saturday; and five for Thursday.

Time to Celebrate

In this section, you will learn how to sign the seasons, as well as a few of the holidays appropriate to the seasons. Visualizing changes that occur during the seasons will help you memorize these sign formations. For instance, during the summer it is very hot, so visualize what happens when you are perspiring. You need to wipe the sweat off your brow when forming this sign.

The signs for "thanks" and "give" can also be blended to represent Thanksgiving. The sign for Hanukkah is made by representing a menorah. Position your hands side by side with palms facing you. All your fingers are in a vertical open position with thumbs tucked into the palms. Then separate your hands.

The sign for Christmas has at least twelve variations. The sign you would select to represent Christmas may depend on where you live as well as on your specific beliefs. Here are descriptions of how to form a few of these variations on the sign for Christmas:

- An arcing "C" moves left to right in front of the body.
- First, pull an imaginary beard from your chin with one hand. Second, using both flat hands, mime-sign the shape of a Christmas tree.
- First, with a "C" hand, tap the chin indicating the beard. Second, move the hand downward indicating Santa's large belly.
- Tap the middle finger of each hand once into the opposite palms. This sign indicates "Jesus." Next, cross the arms at the wrists with "S" hands, then break away. This sign indicates "saves."

You are rounding the bend into February, just in time to celebrate Valentine's Day. You have already learned the "I love you" sign, and now you can combine this with the sign for "heart." This sign can also be made with "Vs" while you outline the heart to represent Valentine's Day.

Time to Celebrate

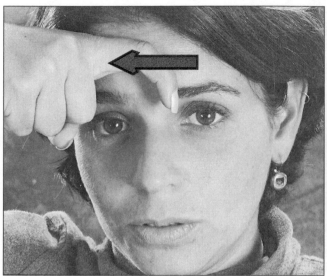

▲ **SUMMER:** To sign "summer," use the "X" hand and drag it across the forehead.

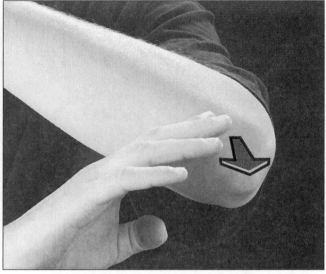

▲ **FALL, AUTUMN:** To sign "fall" or "autumn," brush the arm and elbow, imitating a barren tree, as shown.

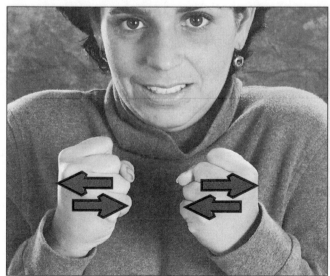

▲ **WINTER:** To sign "winter," shake the "S" hands. It is cold outside, and this makes you shiver. Think of feeling cold when forming this sign.

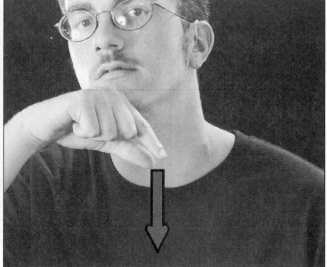

▲ **THANKSGIVING:** This particular sign for "Thanksgiving" indicates the turkey's wattle. To sign "Thanksgiving," shake and lower the "Q" hand under the chin.

Time to Celebrate

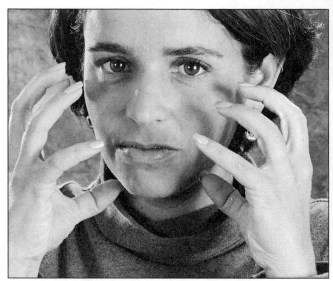

▲ **SANTA:** To sign "Santa," using both "curved five" hands, mime Santa's large beard.

▲ **HEART:** To sign "heart," use both index fingers, or the "touch" classifier to trace the heart starting at the top, then moving around and down.

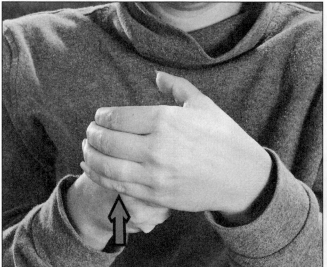

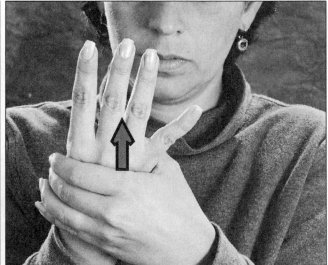

▲ **SPRING, GROW:** This sign represents the growth that occurs during spring. Push the right hand up through the fist of the left hand.

There are two days in spring that have special meaning for many people: Mother's Day and Father's Day. You have already learned the signs for "mother" and "father," and you just finished learning the sign for "day." Simply combine these signs.

Additional Variations

As you know, several signs can be formed in more than one way, including the signs for "now" or "present" and "fall" or "autumn." A variation of the sign for "fall" or "autumn" is to imitate leaves falling to the ground. Use both "open five" hands, palms facing down. Start high, and float your "open five" hands back and forth and downward.

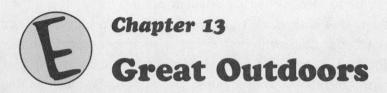

Chapter 13

Great Outdoors

The great outdoors gives us a perfect sign language lesson. You can go for a walk and, while enjoying the fresh air, see and practice what you have just learned. This chapter will introduce you to the signs for different animals, weather, and some of nature's finest elements.

Service Dogs

When the subject of animals comes up, one cannot omit the wonderful work of service animals. These animals are service dogs, guide dogs, hearing dogs, social dogs, and many other types of specially trained dogs. They provide assistance to many different types of individuals, such as the blind, deaf, physically challenged, and more.

A hearing dog is specially trained for the deaf and hard of hearing. Hearing dogs alert their owners to sounds, such as a knock on the door, a doorbell, alarm clocks, a baby crying, a whistling teakettle, a smoke alarm, and many other sounds. The hearing dog acts as the ears for its owner.

Have you ever stepped out into a busy parking lot and moved quickly out of harm's way because you *heard* a vehicle approaching? A hearing dog is trained to alert his owner to just such a danger and more. The peace of mind that hearing dogs can bring to their owners, such as late-deafened adults, is difficult to measure.

FACT

These dogs and their owners work together as a team. Therefore, both the owner and service dog have full rights under the ADA to enter into all places of business where customers are allowed. The assistance that service dogs provide to their owners is invaluable.

Service dogs are not pets. They are working animals, and while these dogs are wearing their special collars, coats, and identifications (usually of a bright orange color), you should never reach out to pet them. Before attempting to give them any special attention, you must request permission from the owner. It is improper to interfere with these dogs when they are working and providing for the needs of their owner.

The Menagerie

Animal signs are a delight to learn, as they are often iconic. In this chapter, you have the opportunity to apply the classifiers that you have just learned and combine them with this new group of sign vocabulary. After studying the new vocabulary, you will be able to use classifiers as an enhancer, giving you a wonderful way to show movement. As an example, you can combine the classifier sign for "travel" with the animal sign for "lion." This combination of a classifier and a sign demonstrates that the lion is moving. When you sign "travel" slowly, you can suggest the appearance of a lion crouching. Add the sign for "tree," which you will find in this chapter. Now, simply pluralize tree by signing it multiple times. Voila! You have just added a jungle. Sounds like fun, and it is!

▲ **ANIMAL:** To sign "animal," place the fingertips of both hands on the chest and rock the hands back and forth, imitating an animal breathing.

Animal Signs

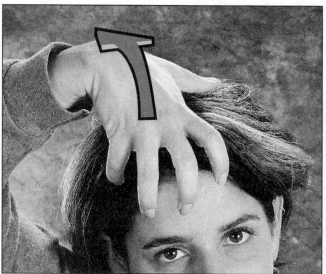

▲ **LION:** To sign "lion," pull the "curved five" hand back over the head, imitating a lion's mane.

▲ **TIGER:** To sign "tiger," use both "curved" hands placed on both sides of the cheeks and draw them apart several times, imitating a tiger's stripes.

▲ **BEAR:** To sign "bear," cross the arms at the wrists and move the hands downward, imitating clawing.

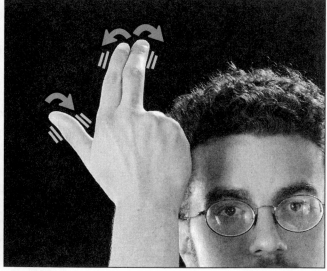

▲ **RABBIT:** To sign "rabbit," place the extended thumb, index, and middle finger near the forehead and wiggle all three fingers. Two hands may also be used to create the sign for "rabbit," adding animation.

Animal Signs

 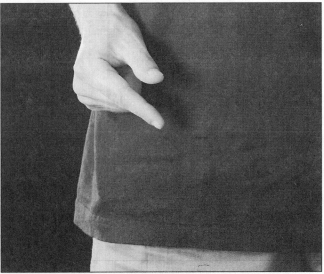

▲ **DOG:** When you sign "dog," the movement and position of the sign represents your dog being obedient and heeling at your side. Snap the "D" hand into the "G" hand.

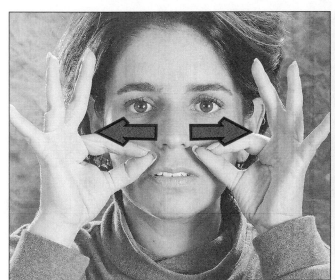 

▲ **CAT:** To sign "cat," move the "F" hands from each side of the mouth outward, imitating a cat's whiskers.

▲ **COW:** To sign "cow," place the thumb of the "Y" hand at the temple and twist. This sign can be made with two hands, imitating the cow's horns.

Animal Signs

▲ **HORSE:** To sign "horse," place the "H" hand on the side of the head and flick back and forth, imitating the ears flicking.

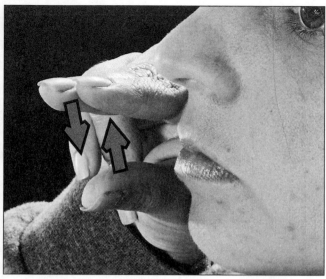

▲ **DUCK:** To sign "duck," place the index, middle, and thumb at the side of the mouth. Open and close your fingers, imitating the beak on a duck.

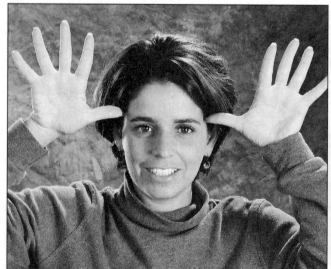

▲ **DEER:** To sign "deer," place the thumbs of both "open five" hands at the temples, imitating antlers.

▲ **SNAKE:** To sign "snake," move the bent "V" hand forward in a variable movement, imitating a snake.

The Weatherman

The morning news comes on, and the weatherman announces it is going to be cold today. There will be rain with lightning changing to snow, and the roads will be slick and icy. Your family member is flying out the door, and you want to warn him the roads may be slippery. In just a moment, you will be able to sign this from the doorway as he's getting in the car. The added communication benefits that come with long-distance signing are yet another great reason to learn sign language.

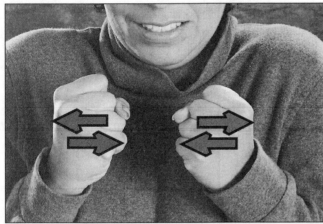

◀ **WINTER, COLD:** To sign "winter" or "cold," shake the "S" hands.

▲ **LIGHTNING:** To sign "lightning," use the index finger and trace a downward zigzag movement, imitating a lightning bolt.

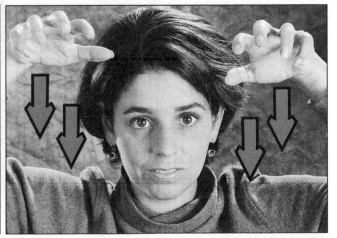

▲ **RAIN:** To sign "rain," use curved "open five" hands and drop the hands in a downward movement several times, imitating the falling rain.

Weather Signs

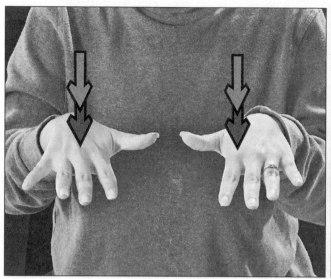 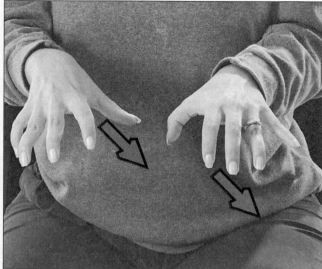

▲ **ICE:** To sign "ice," use both "open five" hands, drop them straight down to "claw" hands, then abruptly stop and slide forward, imitating rain freezing into ice.

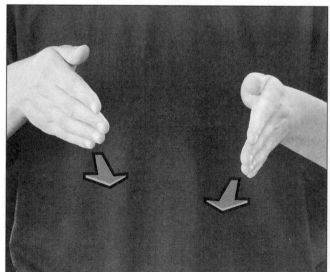 

▲ **ROAD, STREET:** To sign "road" or "street," move "flat" hands forward, palms facing each other, imitating a path, road, or street.

▲ **SUN:** To sign "sun," trace a clockwise circle with the index finger above the head.

Weather Signs

◄ **WIND, BREEZE:** To sign "wind" or "breeze," sweep the "open five" hands side to side in front of the body. The intensity with which you move your hands back and forth in front of your body will indicate the wind's gentleness or its ferocity.

▲ **SKY:** To sign "sky," place the palms facing, hands vertical, then cross hands and arms above the head in an arched movement and spread arms open.

▲ **CLOUD, FOG:** To sign "cloud" or "fog," make a swirling motion with both "claw" hands. The sign for cloud is made high above the head. If you lower the sign to about waist high, it then becomes fog.

Nature's Best

If you are a nature lover or photographer, or if you just like to walk in the woods, you will appreciate these signs.

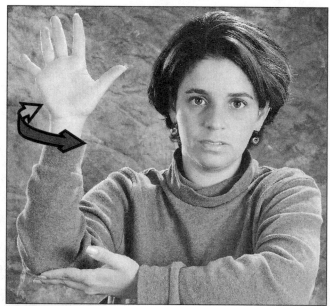

◀ **TREE:** To sign "tree," begin with the elbow resting on the back of the left hand, held in front of the body. Use an "open five" hand, palm facing forward, and pivot the wrist back and forth repeatedly.

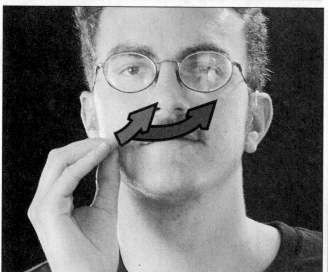

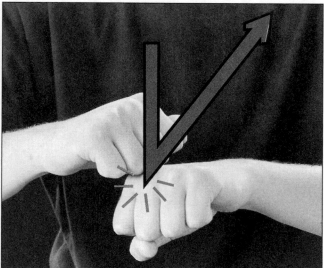

▲ **FLOWER:** To sign "flower," gently tap the "O" hand under the right nostril and then the left. This sign and movement imitates smelling flowers.

▲ **ROCK:** To sign "rock," strike the "closed" right fist on the back of the "closed" left fist.

Nature Signs

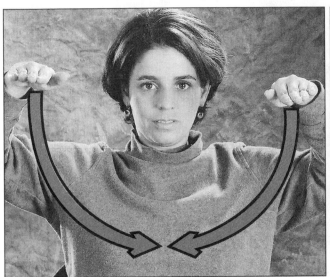

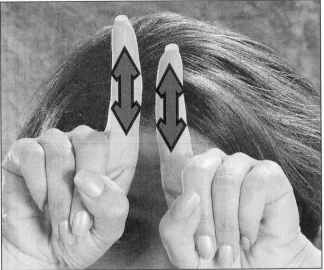

▲ **VALLEY:** To sign "valley," move the "flat" hands downward in a curved movement from the shoulder level until they meet at waist level, imitating the shape of a valley.

▲ **STARS:** To sign "stars," alternate the index fingers up and down.

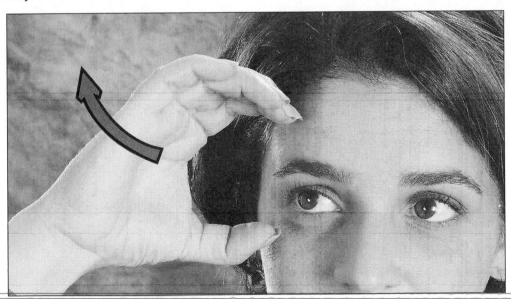

▲ **MOON:** To sign "moon," place the "C" hand at the side of the eye and then swing upward, imitating a quarter moon.

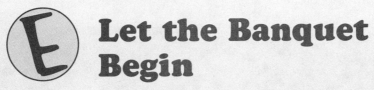

Chapter 14

Let the Banquet Begin

Cooking and eating are two of America's favorite activities. In this chapter, the signs for foods and related items are also bountiful. It is here that you will learn to make the signs for some of your favorite foods. So, let the banquet begin!

Don't Skip Breakfast

It's time to eat. We need to look at food selections and plan the menu for the day. We'll start with breakfast, then move on to lunch, dinner, and, of course, dessert. Along with learning the signs for foods, signs are also presented for cooking techniques and for the other items found in and around the kitchen.

▲ **FOOD, EAT:** To sign "food," tap the lips with a flattened "O" hand in a bouncy movement, imitating eating. To sign "eat," do the same but with a much more steady movement.

You learned in Chapter 12 how to make the various signs that represent time. In this chapter, you will combine these time signs with other signs. The first sign, "breakfast," is an example of this kind of combination sign.

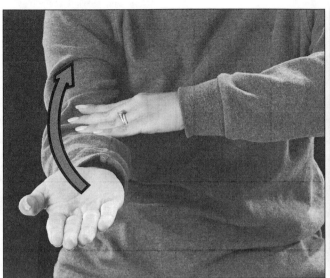

▲ **BREAKFAST:** You will sign "morning" and "eat," and with these two signs together, you create the sign for "breakfast."

The day gets off to a better start with a good breakfast. Would you like to have bacon, eggs, and sausage? These can be served with a little jam or jelly and a banana. Of course, what would the morning be without coffee and orange juice? Here are the signs for breakfast selections.

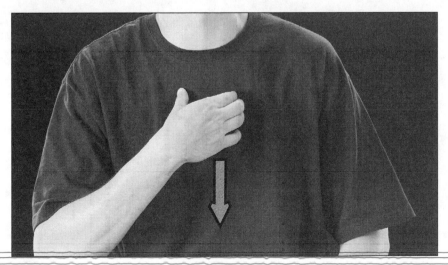

▲ **HUNGRY:** To sign "hungry," draw the "C" hand down the center of the chest once, imitating a hollow feeling.

Breakfast Selections

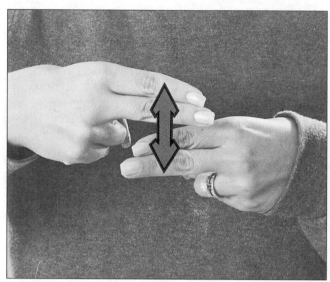

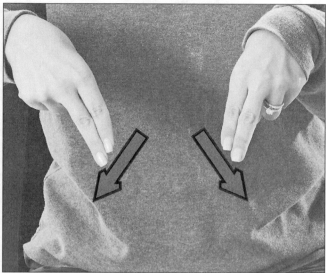

▲ **EGGS:** To sign "eggs," strike the two "H" hands together, then slightly spread them apart, imitating breaking an egg.

▲ **BACON:** To sign "bacon," touch the tips of both "U" hands, palms down, and draw them apart with a wiggle, imitating bacon sizzling in a pan.

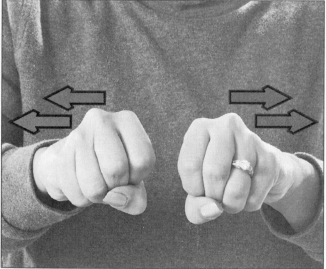

▲ **SAUSAGE:** To sign "sausage," squeeze both "S" hands, while pulling them apart, imitating making sausage.

Breakfast Selections

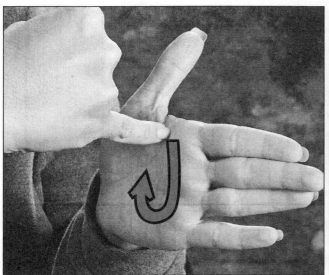

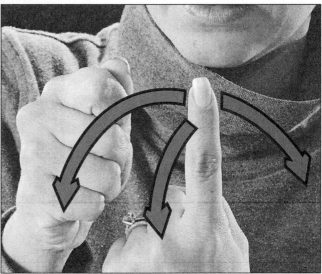

▲ **JAM, JELLY:** To sign "jam" or "jelly," trace the letter "J" into the left "open" palm, imitating spreading jelly.

▲ **BANANA:** To sign "banana," hold the left index finger in an upright, stationary position, then with the right hand make the motion of peeling a banana.

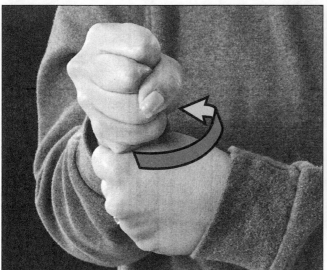

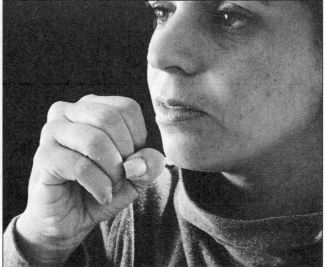

▲ **COFFEE:** To sign "coffee," hold an imaginary cup and rotate the right "S" hand counterclockwise above, imitating turning a coffee grinder.

▲ **ORANGE JUICE:** To sign "orange juice," squeeze the "S" hand near the corner of the mouth, imitating the squeezing of an orange.

Lunchtime!

Now it's time to learn the foods we eat at noontime, otherwise known as lunch, and then we will move on to dinner. "Lunch" is signed in the same manner that you just signed "breakfast."

▲ **LUNCH:** To sign "lunch," you sign "noon" and "eat," and together these two signs create the sign for "lunch."

We have a few light selections, such as soup and a sandwich with a nice glass of milk. Ahh, but then again, you could always slip away to one of those fast-food restaurants! Here, you could order a mouthwatering hamburger with cheese, tomato, onion, and mayonnaise, and a large soda. Of course, if you are going to go that far, you will have to have that extra-large order of french fries.

Lunch Selections

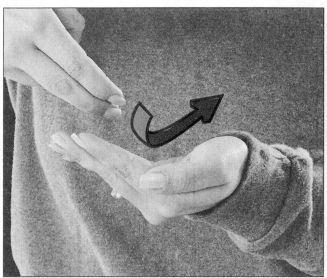

▲ **SOUP:** To sign "soup," dip the right "H" hand, curved like a spoon, into the open left palm, imitating eating a bowl of soup.

▲ **SANDWICH:** To sign "sandwich," bring the "flat" hands, palm-to-palm, toward the mouth, imitating eating a sandwich.

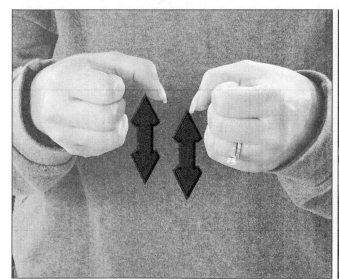

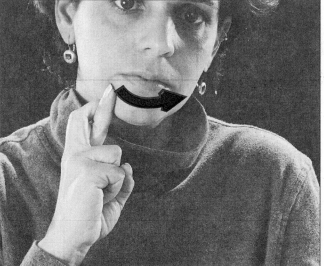

▲ **MILK:** To sign "milk," squeeze one or both "S" hands alternately up and down imitating milking a cow. This sign may also be formed using just one hand.

▲ **RESTAURANT:** To sign "restaurant," tap the "R" hand once on each side of the mouth.

Lunch Selections

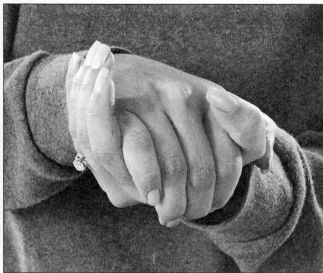

▲ **HAMBURGER:** To sign "hamburger," clasp both "curved" hands and then reverse direction, imitating making a hamburger patty.

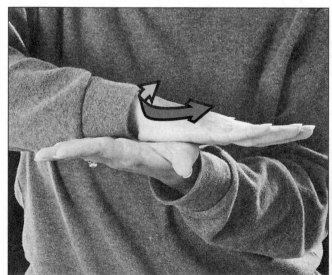

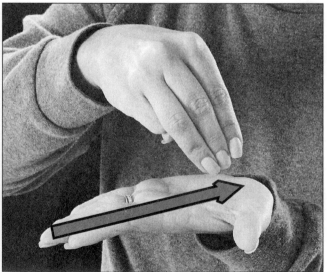

▲ **CHEESE:** To sign "cheese," press the heel of each hand together, twisting back and forth, imitating pressing cheese.

▲ **MAYONNAISE:** To sign "mayonnaise," draw the "M" hand across the left "open" palm, imitating spreading mayonnaise.

Lunch Selections

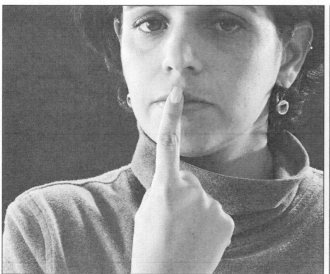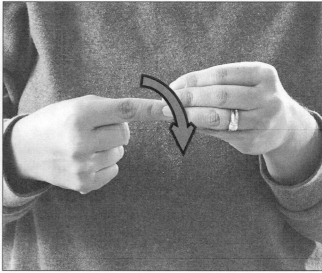

▲ **TOMATO:** To sign "tomato," first sign "red." Then strike the left fingertips with the index finger imitating dicing a tomato.

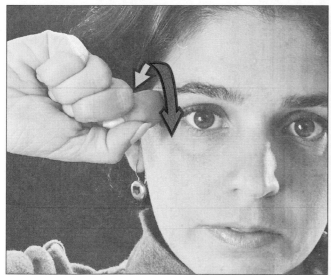

▲ **ONION:** To sign "onion," twist the knuckle of the "S" hand in the corner of eye, imitating the way onions make you cry.

▲ **FRENCH FRIES:** To sign "french fries," slide the "F" hand to the right in two small movements in the fingerspelling position.

Lunch Selections

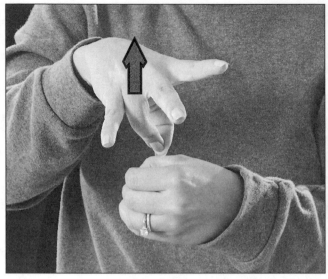 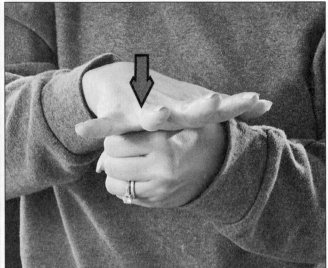

▲ **SODA:** To sign "soda," the left hand holds an imaginary can. The right hand pulls the ring on the top of the can, and then hits the top of the can with the palm, making a "pop" sound. The "soda" sign can also be made by simply signing the last half of the instructions.

ALERT!

Daily practice is very important! One of the ways you can keep up with a daily practice routine is to fingerspell your grocery list items before you write them down. Remember to include brand names in your practice

Afternoon Snack

It is late afternoon, the low point of the day. You have been working hard, and you deserve a little break. It's time for tea, cookies, and fruit. Or perhaps you want a piece of candy. Just remember, it is better for you to eat fruit, such as a peach, pear, or a melon. Another delightful snack is to take fresh strawberries and sprinkle them with sugar. Mmm, delicious!

Afternoon Snack Selections

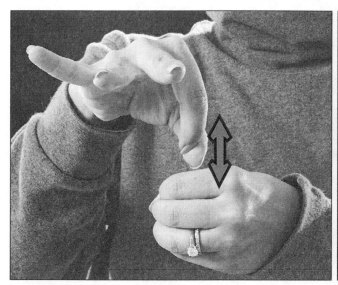

▲ **TEA:** To sign "tea," hold an imaginary cup and dip the "F" hand in and out, imitating dipping a tea bag.

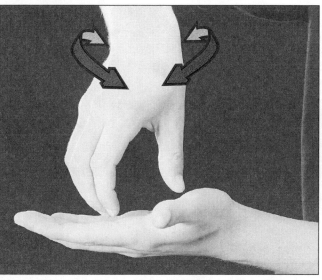

▲ **COOKIE:** To sign "cookie," twist the "C" hand fingertips back and forth on the left "open" palm, imitating cutting out cookies.

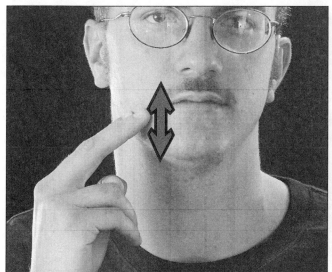

▲ **GUM:** To sign "gum," brush the "U" hand downward over lips and chin several times, imitating wiping drool.

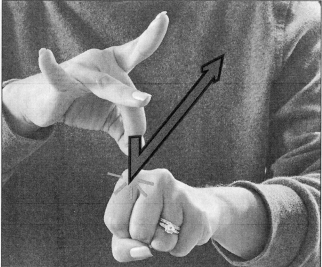

▲ **MELON, PUMPKIN:** To sign "melon" or "pumpkin," flick the middle finger off the back of the stationary left fist, imitating checking the ripeness of a melon.

Afternoon Snack Selections

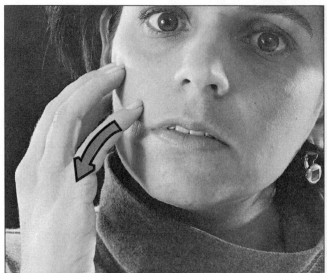
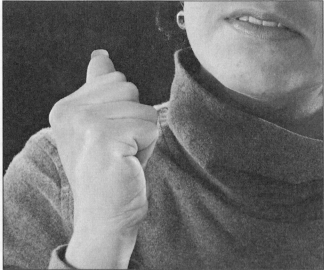

▲ **PEACH:** To sign "peach," place the "curved five" hand on the cheek, then pull away to form a closed "A" hand.

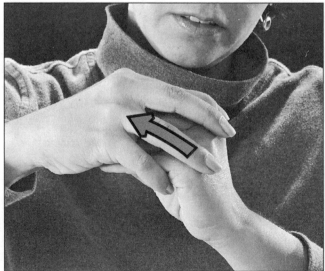

▲ **PEAR:** To sign "pear," cover the left stationary fist with the right hand, then pull away, imitating pulling a pear off a tree.

Afternoon Snack Selections

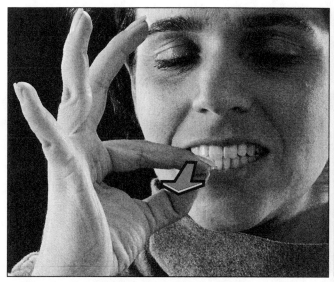

▲ **STRAWBERRIES:** To sign "strawberries," pull the "F" hand away from the teeth, imitating pulling the stem off a strawberry.

▲ **SUGAR, SWEET:** To sign "sugar" or "sweet," stroke the fingertips of the "flat" hand off the chin.

Take a few minutes to review the signs before making a meal or setting the table. Then, just before you handle that item, see if you can remember how to sign it.

The Evening Meal

It is time for dinner. Perhaps this evening we will stay in and cook. We'll go into the kitchen, look inside the refrigerator, and see what there is to eat. It appears the selections for dinner are meat, baked potato, and fish. Then again, it would be simple to just boil some spaghetti, and serve it with bread and butter. In the meantime, while dinner is cooking, we will set the table.

Dinner Selections

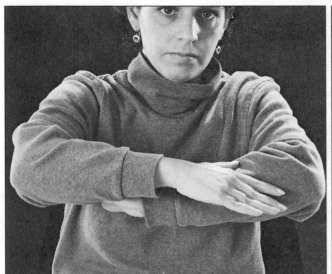 

▲ **DINNER:** You will sign "night" and "eat," and together these two signs create the sign for "dinner."

▲ **REFRIGERATOR:** To sign "refrigerator," hold both arms against the sides of the body and shake the "R" hands gently, imitating cold.

Dinner Selections

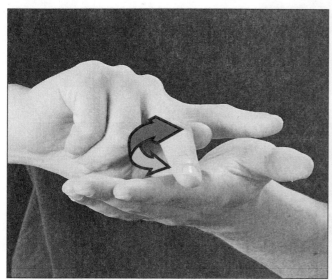

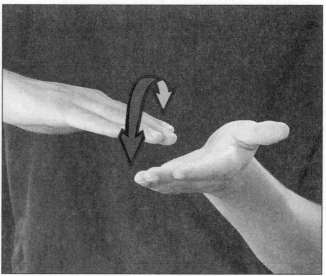

▲ **KITCHEN:** To sign "kitchen," flip the "K" hand back and forth on the palm of the stationary left hand.

▲ **COOK, FRY:** To sign "cook" or "fry," flip the "flat" hand back and forth on the palm of the stationary left hand, imitating cooking.

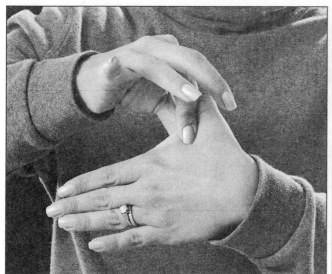

▲ **MEAT:** To sign "meat," use the index finger and thumb to pinch the meaty part of the left hand between the thumb and the index finger.

▲ **OVEN, BAKE:** To sign "oven" or "bake," slide the "flat" hand, palm down, under the left "flat" hand, imitating sliding a pan into an oven.

Dinner Selections

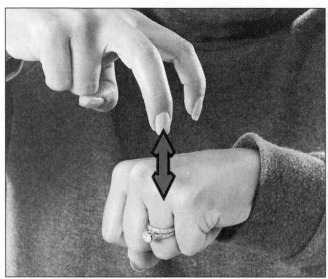

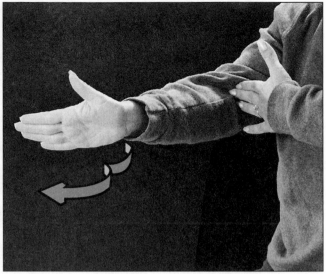

▲ **POTATOES:** To sign "potatoes," tap the curved "V" hand on the back of the left fist, imitating piercing a baked potato.

▲ **FISH:** To sign "fish," move the extended arm, palm facing left, forward in a wiggling motion, imitating a swimming fish.

▲ **BOIL, COOK:** To sign "boil" or "cook," wiggle the fingers of the "curved five" hand under the left palm, imitating water boiling.

▲ **SPAGHETTI:** To sign "spaghetti," touch the tips of both "I" hands, and pull them apart in a circular motion.

Dinner Selections

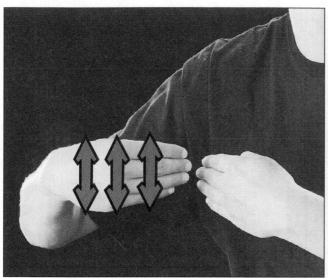

▲ **BREAD:** To sign "bread," move the "flat" hand fingertips up and down in front of the left hand, imitating slicing bread.

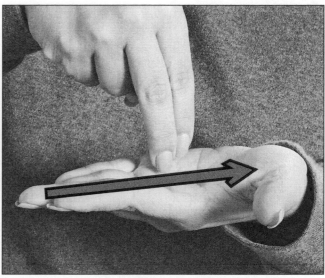

▲ **BUTTER:** To sign "butter," draw the "N" hand across the left "open" palm, imitating spreading butter.

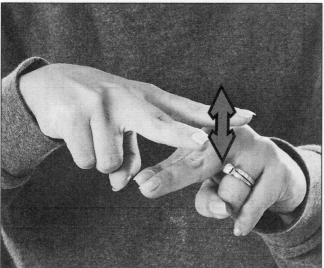

▲ **SALT:** To sign "salt," tap the extended index and middle fingers of the right hand on the extended index and middle fingers of the left hand.

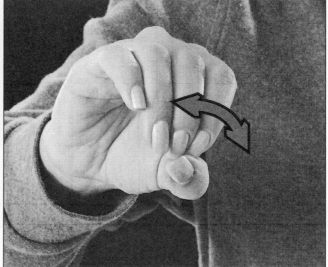

▲ **PEPPER:** To sign "pepper," imitate holding a pepper shaker and shake gently.

Dinner Selections

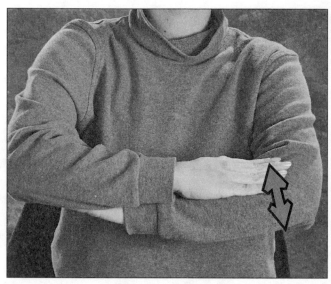

▲ **TABLE:** To sign "table," place both arms across the front of the body, right on top of left, palms facing down, and tap the right palm at the left elbow, imitating a tabletop.

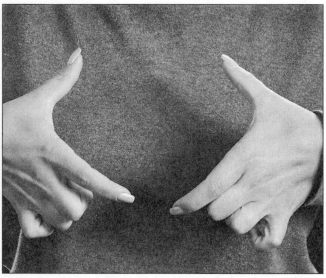

▲ **PLATE:** To sign "plate," use the thumb and index finger of each hand to imitate making the shape of a thin plate.

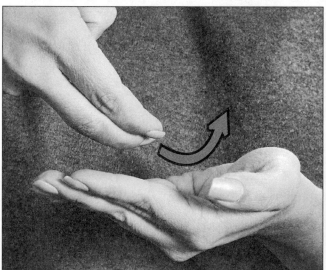

▲ **SPOON:** To sign "spoon," scoop the "H" hand into the left "open" palm.

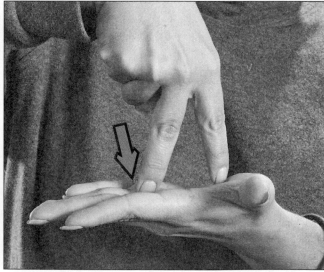

▲ **FORK:** To sign "fork," dig the "V" or "W" hand into the left "open" palm.

Dinner Selections

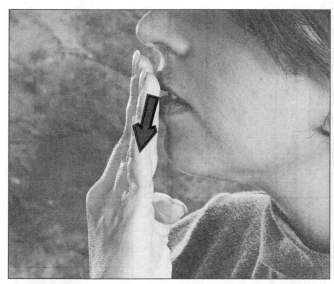

▲ **NAPKIN:** To sign "napkin," use the "flat" palm to wipe the lips.

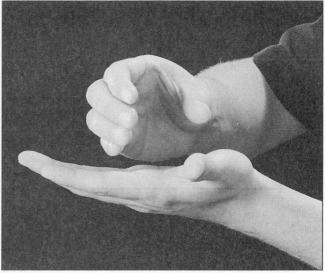

▲ **GLASS:** To sign "glass," use the "C" hand to hold an imaginary glass.

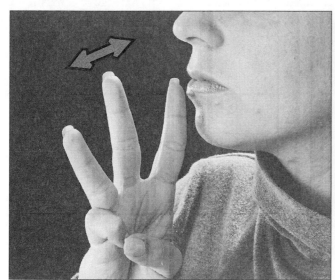

▲ **WATER:** To sign "water," tap the "W" hand on the lips.

▲ **WINE:** To sign "wine," stroke the "W" hand on the cheek in a circular motion, imitating the blush wine can bring to the face.

Sweet Temptations

Now, it's time for the finale! A dessert is a delicious reward when you finish your meat and potatoes, and you've certainly earned such a treat after the meat and potatoes of this chapter! The selections from the dessert menu are cake, pie, and ice cream.

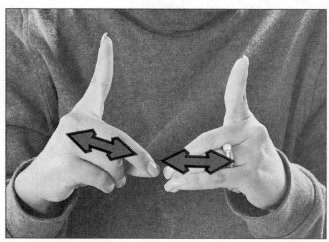

▲ **DESSERT:** To sign "dessert," touch the fingertips of the "D" hands several times.

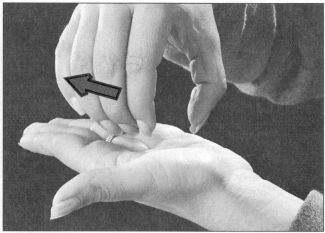

▲ **CAKE:** To sign "cake," pull the "C" hand across the left "open" palm, imitating pulling out a slice of cake.

▲ **PIE:** To sign "pie," use the "flat" hand to slice an imaginary piece of pie in the left "open" palm.

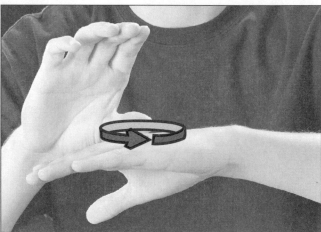

▲ **CHOCOLATE:** To sign "chocolate," circle the "C" hand on the back of the left hand.

Dessert Selections

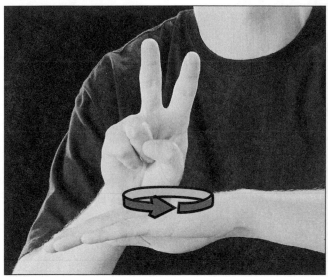

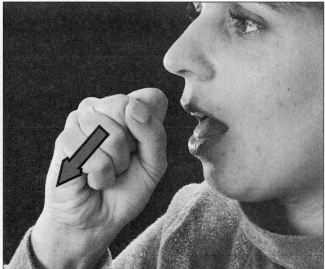

▲ **VANILLA:** To sign "vanilla," circle the "V" hand on the back of the left hand.

▲ **ICE CREAM:** To sign "ice cream," lick an imaginary ice cream cone.

In order to keep these sixty-five food signs clear in your memory, sign them every chance you get. Try to remember the importance of practice. The very next time you sit down for a meal, sign, sign, and sign everything you see on the table.

Imagine it is the end of the day and you are planning to unwind. Pop some popcorn, and pour yourself a drink before you settle in front of the television for a while. Fingerspell the letters "T" and "V"; this makes the "loan" sign for "television/TV." To form the sign for a drink of Seven Up, first sign the number 7, then with the index finger, point upwards. Make this combination of these two signs as smooth as possible. Learning to combine and execute two or more signs smoothly gets you well underway to becoming a good signer.

Dessert Selections

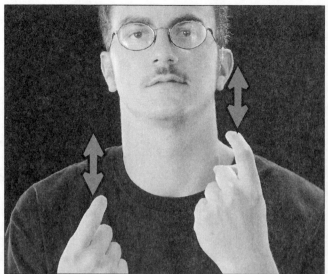

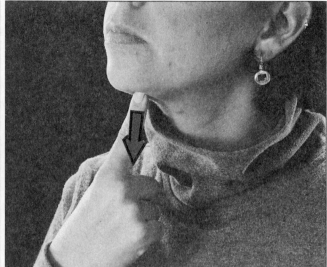

▲ **POPCORN:** To sign "popcorn," flick both index fingers alternately, imitating popping corn.

▲ **THIRSTY:** To sign "thirsty," stroke the index finger down the throat.

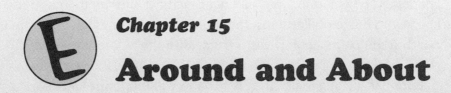

Chapter 15

Around and About

Look around the living room at home and you will probably see a television and the telephone—two things that are taken for granted in most homes. In this chapter, we will look into learning how to sign items around the house and at work, and we will learn a little bit more about captioned television programs and the TTY/TDD.

Home Sweet Home

American Sign Language is really all about describing. When it comes to describing things around the house, there seems to be one particular handshape that is used repeatedly. This handshape is the "flat" hand, also known as the "modified B" hand. So, what's a "modified B"? The letter "B" is formed with all fingers vertical and the thumb in the palm. The key to this modification is the thumb. Using a "modified B," the thumb is not in the palm, but instead is flat against the side of the hand. The use of this handshape provides the signer with accuracy for describing things that are flat. Putting to use the "flat" hand will empower you as a signer. As you acquire the following vocabulary for things around the house, you will see the power of the flat hand in the signs again and again.

Things Around the House

▲ **HOME:** To sign "home," tap the fingertips of the flat "O" hand to the corner of the mouth, then open to a flat palm against the cheek.

Things Around the House

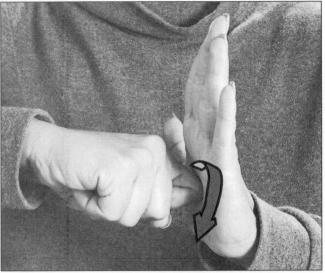

▲ **HOUSE:** To sign "house," touch the fingertips of the "flat" hands, imitating the roof of a house.

▲ **KEY:** To sign "key," turn the knuckle of the index finger into the left, vertical, "open" palm, imitating locking a door.

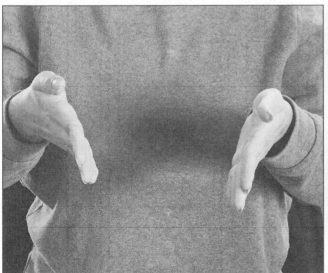

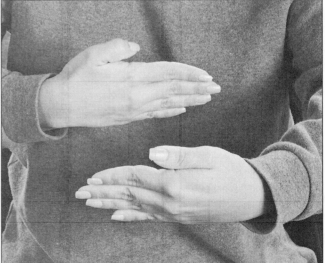

▲ **ROOM:** To sign "room," use both "flat" hands and move them in a box shape to indicate two sets of walls: front and back, and both sides.

Things Around the House

▲ **BEDROOM:** To sign "bedroom," place both hands, palm to palm, on the side of the face, imitating sleep. Then sign "room."

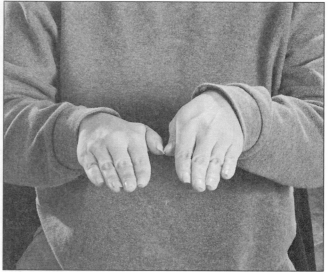

▲ **FLOOR:** To sign "floor," use the "flat" hands, palms down, thumbs touching, then separate them, imitating a flat surface.

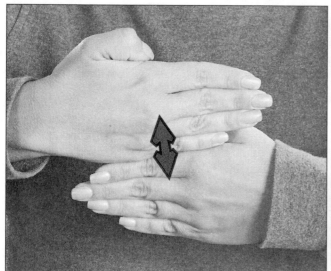

▲ **WINDOW:** To sign "window," use "flat" hands, and with the right hand on top of the left hand, raise the right hand, imitating opening a window.

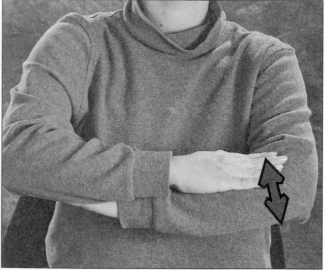

▲ **TABLE:** To sign "table," place both arms across the front of the body, right on top of left, palms facing down, and tap the right palm at the left elbow, imitating a tabletop.

Concluding our list are two items that are fingerspelled and are considered "loan" signs.

1. "Air conditioning" is signed "AC."
2. "Television" is signed "TV."

FACT

There are a few different variations of the sign for "home." For instance, you can tap the fingertips of the flat "O" hand to the corner of the mouth, then on the cheek. Or you can tap the fingertips of the flat "O" hand twice near the cheek.

The Telephone and the TTY

We use the phone daily for our communication needs, and so do the deaf. Unlike regular phones, the deaf and hard of hearing use phones that are referred to as TTYs/TDDs. The TTY is a text telephone system. It has a keyboard, a small screen, and an optional printer. It works through an ordinary telephone line.

Today, due to ADA mandates, the availability of TTYs has increased. These mandates have provided the deaf and hard-of-hearing population with improved access to communication. Some of the service providers affected by these mandates include hospitals, police departments, fire departments, schools, airports, and hotels.

FACT

In 1964, Robert H. Weitbrecht, a deaf man, invented an electronic device called the acoustic coupler. The coupler enabled typewritten communication over the phone with the use of a teletypewriter.

If you work in any of the listed areas that are mandated to have TTYs, don't be afraid to use it. TTYs are user friendly. However, be aware that a TTY user can only make direct calls to another TTY user.

Abbreviations Often Used

Many abbreviations are often used during a TTY conversation. Here are a few of the basic abbreviations.

Word	Abbreviation
Are	R
Because	CUZ
Go ahead	GA
Hold	HD
Oh, I see	OIC
Operator	OPR
Please	PLS
Question mark	Q
See you later	CUL
Should	SHD
Stop keying	SK
Thanks	THX
Tomorrow	TMW
You	U
Yours	UR

Relay Telephone Service

If a person does not own a TTY and needs to contact a deaf TTY user or vice versa, a relay telephone service must be used. You can dial the number 711 for the relay telephone service in your state. This is how it all works:

- You, the caller, dial the relay number.
- A relay communication assistant, or CA, answers. The CA is equipped with a TTY.
- You tell the CA the TTY number you wish to call.
- The CA then uses the keyboard on their TTY and dials that number.

- You tell the CA what you would like communicated through the TTY. The CA will then become the voice of the deaf person by reading the typed text that comes in reply to your end of the conversation.
- A CA relay operator will always speak in the first person when reading from their TTY.
- You must also speak as if you are speaking directly to the person they called.
- During a relay call, only one person can speak or type at a time.
- Both parties must say or type "Go Ahead" or "GA" to indicate it is the other person's turn to speak or type.

Technological Advances

Today, technological advances have certainly assisted in filling some of the communication gaps that the deaf have faced over many years. These advances include the use of e-mail, instant messaging, text pagers, and compact portable TTYs. There are even visual phones that are available, though they are not yet perfected. In the near future, we can look forward to visual phones that will be able to send out images fast enough to allow a "real time" signed conversation.

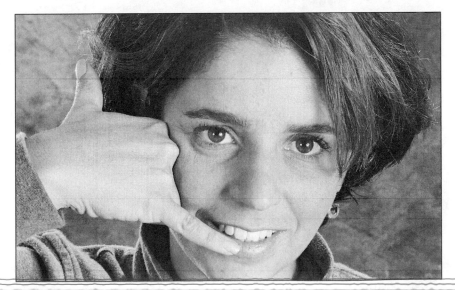

▲ **TELEPHONE:** To sign "telephone," place the "Y" hand up to your ear, imitating talking on a telephone.

School Days

Think back to your early years in elementary school. Visualize your teacher standing in front of the class, *clapping* her hands and saying, "Come on, children, it's time to settle down and put our thinking caps on!" Making visual associations, such as this one, adds clarity to the formation of some signs. Clap your hands twice and you have made the sign for school. Now let's play school and learn additional sign vocabulary.

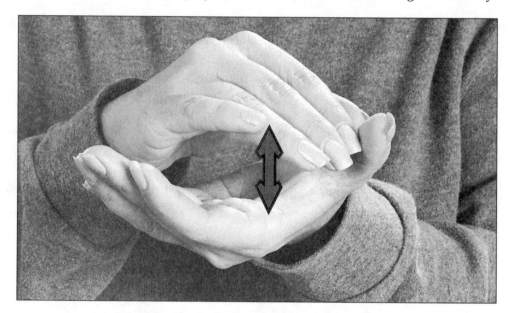

▲ **SCHOOL:** To sign "school," clap your hands twice.

There is a special way to demonstrate the school years, freshman through senior. Tap the right index finger on the appropriate finger of the left "open five" hand, like so:

- **Freshman:** tap the ring finger.
- **Sophomore:** tap the middle finger.
- **Junior:** tap the index finger.
- **Senior:** tap the thumb.

There is a variation in signing school years. Instead of tapping the fingers on the left hand, simply tap your right thumb, index, middle finger, or ring finger into the palm of the left hand.

School Days

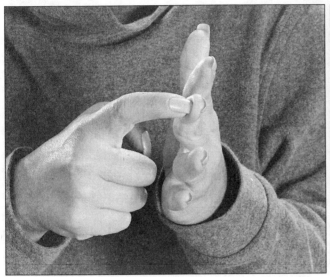

▲ **SOPHOMORE:** To sign "sophomore," tap the right index finger on the middle finger of the left "open five" hand.

▲ **EDUCATION:** To sign "education," use both "E" hands on the sides of the forehead and push forward slightly.

School Subjects

Do you remember your favorite subject in school? Here are five subjects for you to sign.

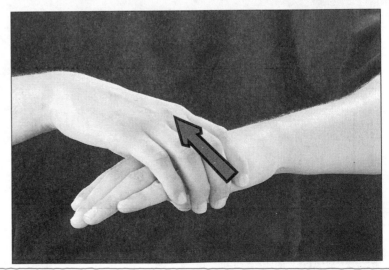

▲ **ENGLISH:** To sign "English," use the right hand to cover the back of the left "flat" hand then pull it toward you.

School Subjects

▲ **MATH:** To sign "math," cross the "M" hands repeatedly.

▲ **SCIENCE:** To sign "science," use both alternating "A" hands, point thumbs down, and make a pouring motion, imitating measuring liquids from science beakers.

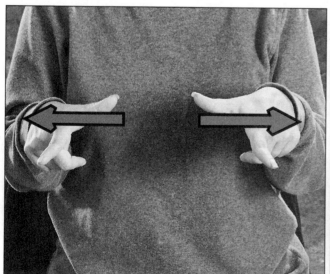

▲ **LANGUAGE:** To sign "language," touch the thumbs of both "L" hands, then separate.

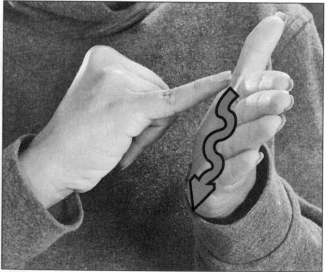

▲ **ART:** To sign "art," use the "I" hand and draw a wavy motion down the left palm, imitating drawing.

Working in Education

Still imagining you are in school, let's continue to further your educational vocabulary. This vocabulary is important for those who work in educational settings. Sit up straight, pay attention, and let's get down to business.

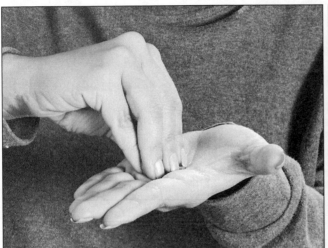

▲ **LEARN:** To sign "learn," place all the fingertips into the left palm. Next, pull upward with a modified "O" hand and place it on the forehead, imitating putting knowledge in the mind.

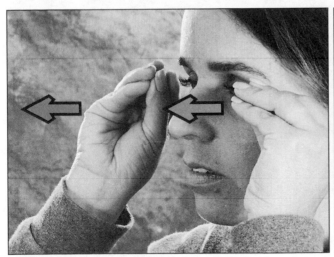
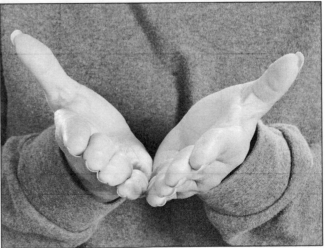

▲ **TEACH:** To sign "teach," place both flat "O" hands at the temples, then push forward, imitating the process of taking knowledge out of the teacher's head and giving it to the students.

▲ **BOOK:** To sign "book," place both "flat" hands, side by side, imitating opening a book.

Educational Vocabulary

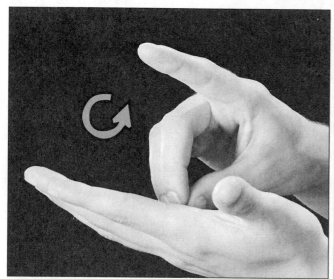

▲ **DICTIONARY:** To sign "dictionary," use the "D" hand and make a circular motion on the left palm, imitating turning pages.

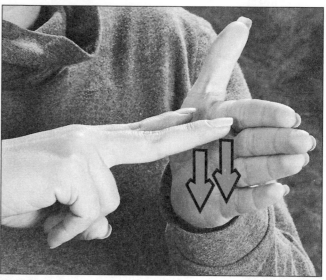

▲ **READ:** To sign "read," use the "V" hand and make a downward motion on the left palm, imitating reading. A second version is to make the motion moving left to right.

▲ **WRITE:** To sign "write," mimic writing on the left palm.

▲ **SENTENCE:** To sign "sentence," interlock the "F" hands, then pull apart, imitating a string of words.

Punctuation

As you know, gesturing and mime are both part of ASL. With that in mind, let's learn how to form punctuation. All of the following punctuation marks are traced in the air exactly as though you were writing them. Remember to make these five punctuation marks large enough so they may easily be seen by the reader.

Punctuation Mark	Symbol
Question mark	?
Exclamation point	!
Quotation marks	" "
Colon	:
Semicolon	;

Educational Vocabulary

▲ **EXAM, TEST:** To sign "exam" or "test," use both hands to trace question marks in the air, then drop your hands to an "open five" hand. Don't forget to add the dots underneath your question marks!

College Years

You are doing so well at this point that it's time to move on to the college level, to graduate, and to get your diploma.

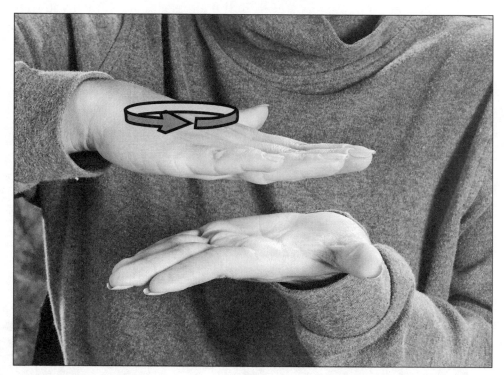

▲ **COLLEGE, UNIVERSITY:** To sign "college" or "university," start with hands touching, then move the dominant hand over and above the other hand. Circle the right "open" palm counterclockwise above the left "open" palm.

Variations for these specific signs often use "initializations" while maintaining the same movement as described above. Here are a few examples:

- **College:** Use the right "C" hand.
- **University:** Use the right "U" hand.
- **Graduate:** Use the right "G" hand.

Educational Vocabulary

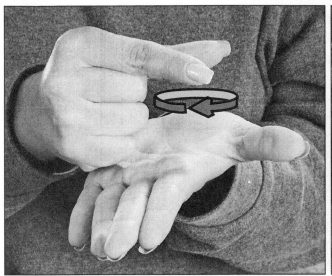

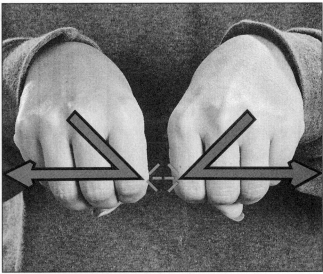

▲ **GRADUATE:** To sign "graduate," form a clockwise circle with the "G" hand in the left open palm.

▲ **DIPLOMA:** To sign "diploma," touch the "O" hands together and draw them apart, imitating the shape of a diploma.

As you progress through the material in these chapters, you should constantly be realizing how important it is to know the handshapes of the letters of the alphabet. A good way to practice fingerspelling is to use this table of abbreviations for specific academic degrees.

Degree	Fingerspelled Abbreviation
Bachelor of arts	B.A.
Bachelor of science	B.S.
Bachelor of science in nursing	B.S.N.
Doctor of dental science	D.D.S.
Doctor of education	Ed.D.
Education specialist	Ed.S.
Juris doctor (law degree)	J.D.
Doctor of medicine	M.D.

Working Nine to Five

Work is described in many different ways because it varies from one person to the other. Whether your job requires going to school full-time, taking care of children, or working as a service provider, it is all described as work. The sign for work has variations that are used to indicate intonation and degree of intensity.

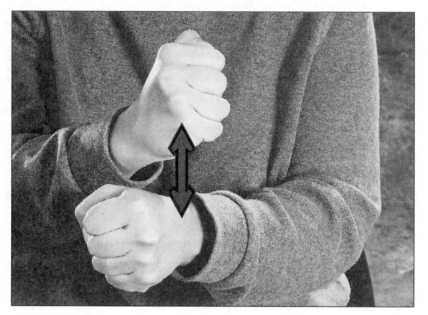

▲ **WORK:** To sign "work," use the right "S" hand to strike the left "S" hand twice.

When signing "work," you can demonstrate how hard you might have worked by increasing the intensity and the speed with which one hand strikes against the other. Suppose you had a rare day at work, and things went smoothly. You can also demonstrate this kind of easy workday by changing the intensity to a slower, softer tapping of the wrists.

So it's off to work we go. The start times and the end times of your job are very important. You've already learned some of the time signs in Chapter 12; therefore, you know how to point to your watch to indicate time. Let's now learn how to sign "start" and "stop."

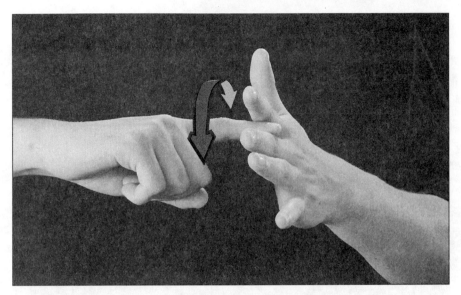

▲ **BEGIN, START:** "Start" is an iconic sign. Visualize placing the key in the ignition of a vehicle and turning it. Place the index finger of the "D" hand between the index and middle finger of the left hand, and turn.

Don't limit the sign "start" just to starting a vehicle. This sign can be combined with many signs you have learned in previous chapters. With this little exercise, you can expand your vocabulary from singles to pairs. Here's how it works. We start with a basic phrase describing a common action. You visualize this action then sign the words that make it into a series of complete sentences. As you sign the words in the sentences, don't be hesitant to throw in a little mime and gesture. Here we go.

You wake up in the morning and then you . . .

- Start getting dressed, making the coffee, and cooking breakfast.
- Start the car and your workday.
- Start to smile, time for a coffee break!

All the words in these three sentences you know how to sign. Just a reminder, you do not need to sign any of the little words we're so used to saying, such as "the," "a," or "to." Visualization is a great tool. Use it, and you will sign successfully.

Working Nine to Five

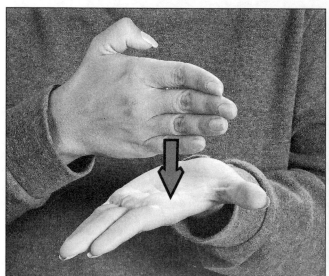

▲ **STOP:** To sign "stop," use the side of the "flat" hand to hit the left "open" palm once.

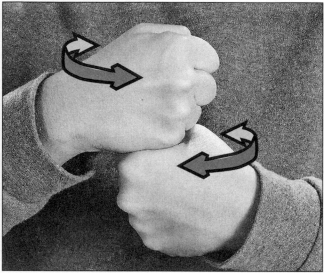

▲ **MAKE:** To sign "make," place "S" hands one on top of the other, then twist back and forth.

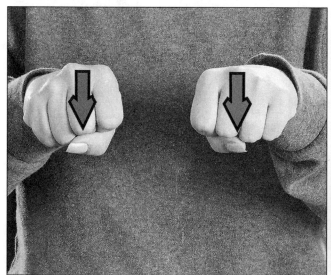

▲ **CAN, ABLE:** To sign "can" (as in "I can") or "able," bend both "S" hands at the wrists and move them downward.

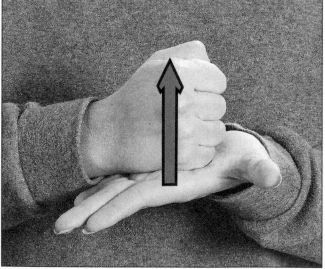

▲ **HELP:** To sign "help," place the "A" hand in the left "open" palm and lift both hands upward.

Working Nine to Five

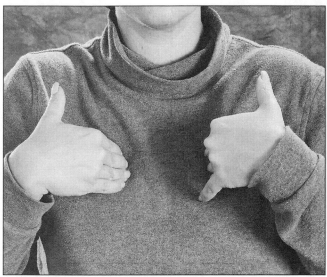

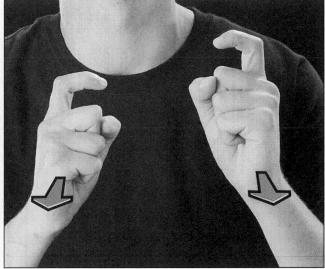

▲ **HAVE:** To sign "have," place the fingertips of both hands against the chest wall.

▲ **GIVE, GIFT, PRESENT:** To sign "give," "gift," or "present," move both "X" hands forward in a giving motion.

As always, you need to practice and apply the new signs you have just learned. If possible, teach a friend or family member these new signs so they can practice with you.

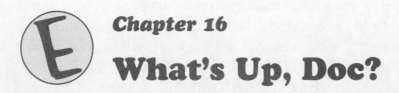

Chapter 16

What's Up, Doc?

This chapter covers all areas of the medical arena. You will be provided with information regarding the special considerations for the deaf and hard of hearing in a medical setting. This chapter also presents communication strategies, as well as the latest information on cochlear implants.

In Sickness and in Health

There are over 22 million deaf and hard of hearing people in the United States. Many of them will need hospital medical or emergency care at some point in their lives. The anxiety associated with this experience is profound. A hearing person can only imagine the distress produced by the soundless images of the emergency room, operating room, recovery room, testing laboratories, medical equipment, and medical personnel in a hurry. Even more apprehension is generated for the deaf and hard of hearing by their fears of being isolated, misunderstood, and their failing to understand questions and instructions.

Today, medical and hospital personnel all possess the ability to alleviate the kinds of problems encountered by the deaf and hard of hearing in medical situations and to deliver effective, quality care to them. Increased awareness, preventive actions, and simple considerations will ease many of the fears and apprehensions that accompany medical and emergency services.

FACT

Knowledge of ASL is the medical community's most effective line of communication. Establishing this mode of communication will help facilitate an accurate and quicker evaluation of a deaf or hard of hearing patient.

In addition to sign language, patients can, or may, use any one of these various methods of communication with medical staff:

- Lip reading
- Writing
- Gesturing and mime
- Use of hearing aids
- Speech
- Use of interpreters

Communication Strategies

To improve interpersonal communication between medical personnel and deaf and hard-of-hearing patients, here is a list of very important communication strategies:

- Speak clearly and in simple sentences, rephrasing rather than repeating.
- Do not exaggerate your lip movements.
- Speak naturally, not too fast, and do not shout.
- Do not turn away in the middle of a sentence.
- Allow more time for communication.
- Do not allow two people to speak at the same time.
- Maintain eye contact by looking directly at the patient's face when speaking.
- Face the light while speaking, eliminating shadows and easing lip reading.
- Use pantomime, gestures, and facial expressions to assist you in communicating.
- Avoid technical terms and jargon.
- Write important messages, such as directions, in simple language.
- Provide an interpreter when the patient is unable to comprehend information.
- Provide an interpreter when an injury or medical problem is complex.
- Speak to the patient, not to the interpreter.

Specific Medical Considerations

Due to unintentional communication barriers, the deaf and hard of hearing often need more support and explanation than is required for other patients. The following suggestions and considerations will help improve communication, minimize difficulties, and ensure that the patient is being provided with effective and caring medical treatment:

- When it is necessary for medical personnel to use hygienic precautions, such as masks that cover the mouth, the use of clear masks should be considered to enable lip reading.

- Patients may need or want to use sign language; therefore, it is important not to restrict the patient's hands or arms. If possible, use the forearm area to insert any intravenous needle, or IV. When placed in the back of the hand or the wrist area, IVs limit hand movement and cause discomfort. (This same rule applies to those patients who are not deaf or hard of hearing but who use sign language as a mode of communication with their family members.)

- Patients who are lying down will have difficulty lip reading. Try to speak from the same level. Only 30 percent of all language can be seen on the lips, even under the best of conditions.

- The face of a patient should not be covered unless necessary. This is due to the importance of sight for comprehension. If vision is compromised for any reason, gentle and constant reassuring touching should be given.

- The patient should not be isolated or left in complete darkness.

- Do not engage in small talk. Although this is reassuring to hearing patients, it may cause deaf or hard of hearing patients to feel that they are missing important information, and they may become agitated and confused.

- Ensure that patients have access to their hearing aids and glasses. These are vital communication tools.

- It is inappropriate to use family members as interpreters in medical situations.

First Aid

Warm up your hands because you're now going to learn a few signs that are appropriate to the medical setting. Your first lesson is an easy one. To sign parts of the anatomy, all you need to do is simply point to the specific body part. See, that wasn't so bad now, was it? Now on to the second lesson.

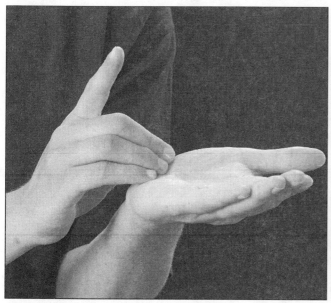

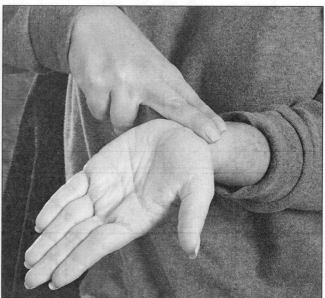

▲ **DOCTOR:** To sign "doctor," place the "D" hand on the inside of the left wrist, imitating taking a pulse.

▲ **NURSE:** To sign "nurse," place the "N" hand on the inside of the left wrist, imitating taking a pulse.

To sign the word "medical," you would form the sign that you made for "doctor" and "nurse," using your "M" hand instead. It would not be unusual to see a deaf or hard-of-hearing patient specifically sign "medical" in reference to a doctor or nurse.

First Aid Signs

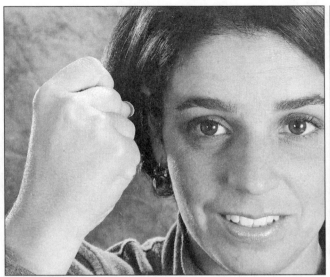

▲ **UNDERSTAND:** To sign "understand," make a fist at the temple, then snap open the index finger to a vertical position.

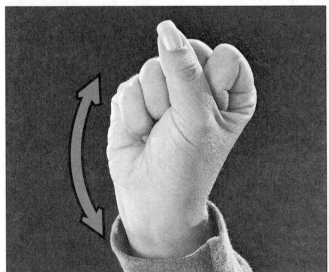

▲ **YES:** To sign "yes," pivot the "S" hand up and down at the wrist.

▲ **NO:** To sign "no," bring the extended thumb, index, and middle fingers together. This is an abbreviated form of the letters "N" and "O."

First Aid Signs

▲ **WRITE:** To sign "write," hold an imaginary pen or pencil and imitate writing onto your left palm.

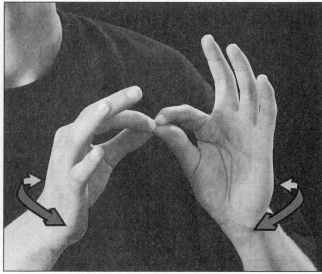

▲ **INTERPRET:** To sign "interpret," hold the "F" hands, palms facing, with thumb and index fingers in contact with each other. Then rotate the hands back and forth.

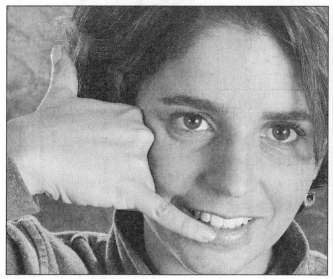

▲ **TELEPHONE:** To sign "telephone," place the "Y" hand to the ear, imitating holding a phone.

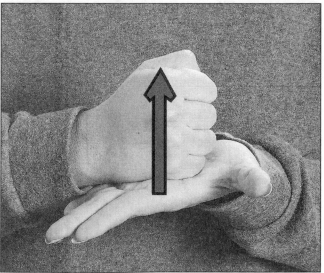

▲ **HELP:** To sign "help," place the "A" hand into the palm of the left hand and raise both hands up.

First Aid Signs

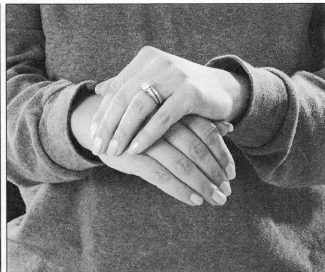

▲ **COMFORTABLE:** To sign "comfortable," stroke the "curved" hands, one on top of the other.

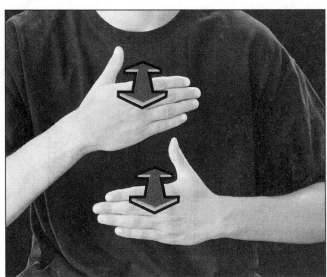

▲ **BREATHE:** To sign "breathe," move both "flat" hands to and from the chest, imitating the movement of breathing.

▲ **HEART:** To sign "heart," use both index fingers or middle fingers to trace the heart starting at the top, then moving around and down.

The "Broken Ear"

The "Broken Ear" is a national symbol that is used to publicly represent deafness and/or services for the deaf and hard of hearing. When this symbol is displayed within a hospital setting, it denotes the presence of a deaf or hard of hearing patient.

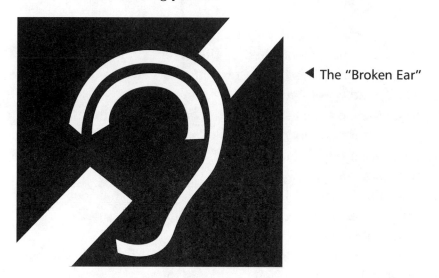

◀ The "Broken Ear"

This symbol should be displayed or attached on the following:

- Admission form
- Patient identification bracelet
- Cover of the patient's chart
- All pertinent records and medical information
- Intercom button at the nurse's station denoting the patient's room
- Head or foot of the patient's bed, with their permission

Deaf and hard of hearing patients, when entering into medical situations, are always appreciative of medical personnel who can communicate in sign. If you are considering a position in the medical field, it would be extremely advantageous to take a sign language course. Hospitals and medical facilities eagerly hire staff members who have knowledge or experience with sign language. Today, hospitals, physician's offices, clinics, and all medical facilities must comply with ADA mandates, making sign language a sought-after skill.

Exploring the Ear

The ear is a small and fascinating precision instrument that is part of our human anatomy. It receives sounds and transmits the information to our brains. But how does it really work? Let's find out by taking this short voyage into the ear.

1. Sound waves carrying environmental noise, speech, and conversations are collected by the outer portion of the ear. These sound waves travel down the ear canal to the eardrum.
2. The sound waves cause the eardrum to vibrate. This in turn sets three ossicle bones—the anvil, the hammer, and the stirrup—in the middle ear into motion. The middle ear acts as a transformer, passing on the vibrations of sounds to the inner portion of the ear, known as the cochlea.
3. The vibration in the inner ear fluid causes the hair cells that line the cochlea to move. The hair cells change this movement into electrical impulses.
4. These electrical impulses are sent up to the brain, via the auditory nerve, where they are interpreted as sound.

When damage occurs to the cochlea, the electrical impulses are not allowed to reach the nerve fibers that are responsible for carrying sound information to the brain.

Signs of Hearing Loss

Approximately 20 million people in the United States are deaf or hard of hearing. Signs of a hearing loss in both adults and children include the following behaviors:

- Saying "huh" or "what" frequently.
- Requesting things to be repeated.
- Turning the volume up on the television or radio.
- Sitting close to the television, with the volume turned up very loud.

- Misunderstanding conversations.
- Becoming confused with words that sound alike.
- Inattentive at home, school, or social gatherings.
- Withdrawn behaviors.
- Turning of the head and leaning, favoring one ear or another.
- Speaking loudly.
- Staring at people who are speaking.
- Answering questions incorrectly.
- Inappropriate speech development.
- Nonverbal.

Definition of Hearing Loss

A general description for deafness is the inability to hear and understand speech. Approximately one-fourth of the population represents this description. Let us look at two definitions of hearing losses.

1. A conductive hearing loss is damage that occurs to the outer or middle ear.
2. Nerve deafness, or sensorineural hearing loss, is damage that has occurred to the tiny hair cells within the cochlea. These damaged hair cells prevent the electrical impulses from reaching the auditory nerve fibers. Therefore, these fibers do not have information to send up to the brain.

The term "hard of hearing" is preferred over "hearing impaired" by the Deaf community and the hard of hearing when referring to individuals who have a hearing loss.

Decibel Ranges

Taking a minute, here is a simple overview of what people hear at various decibel ranges. A decibel, abbreviated as "dB," is a unit of measurement for the loudness of sound.

Decibel Range	Example of a Sound
0–10 dB	Birds tweeting, water dripping
10–20 dB	People whispering, ticking of a clock
20–40 dB	Quiet conversation
40–60 dB	Baby crying, average conversation
60–80 dB	Dog barking, piano playing
80–90 dB	Motorcycle, lawnmower
90–100 dB	Truck, bus
100–110 dB	Helicopter, outboard motor
110–120 dB	Rock band, thunder
120 dB and above	Jet plane, jackhammer, shotgun blast, dynamite

How does all this relate to our ability to hear the spoken word for the purpose of communication? The degree of loss certainly affects speech, the acquisition of language, and the ability to communicate readily. You will hear these descriptions when people are discussing hearing losses:

Decibel Range	Description
0–15 dB	Normal hearing.
16–35 dB	Mild degree of loss. Likely to experience difficulty in communication; may miss 10 percent of speech.
36–50 dB	Moderate degree of loss. Likely to understand conversations within very close range, three to five feet. The probability of missing conversation beyond that range can be as high as 100 percent. Expressive speech may be affected.

(continued) ▶

Decibel Range	Description
51–70 dB	Moderate to severe degree of loss. Conversations must be extremely loud, and in all probability, 100 percent of speech is missed. Language acquisition is delayed, and speech intelligibility is reduced.
71–90 dB	Severe degree of loss. Delayed spontaneous language and speech, and likely to rely on visual communication.
91 dB plus	Profound degree of loss. Speech and oral language acquisition does not develop spontaneously. Speech is likely to be unintelligible. The person relies on vision for communication and learning.

Hearing Aids

The varying degrees of hearing loss provide a general description of what can occur to someone who hears at these levels. These descriptions do not take into account any of the benefits that come from assistive listening amplification systems (or hearing aids). Today there are multiple varieties of hearing aids available. This selection has greatly improved with the advances in hearing technology.

In the 1800s, different sizes and shapes of speaking tubes and ear trumpets were used to amplify sounds. They were held up to the ear and were extremely cumbersome. In the early 1900s, the batteries that powered hearing aids were so large that they were either carried in a box or strapped to the person's leg.

Our present-day technological advances allow hearing aids to make loud sounds softer and soft sounds louder. This improvement alone helps to eliminate the distortion factors that are created when sound is amplified. In addition, hearing aids come in a wide selection of sizes and styles, some of which can be worn in the ear canal or over the ear.

Cochlear Implants

One of the greatest technological advances to date for assistive listening devices has been the invention of the cochlear implant. The cochlear implant was invented in 1972 and was approved by the Federal Drug Administration (FDA) in the mid-1980s. The FDA has approved cochlear implants in adults and children as young as twelve months old. There are three groups of potential candidates for cochlear implants:

- Prelingual deaf children or adults—people who were deafened before acquiring speech.
- Postlingual deaf children or adults—people whose hearing was lost after acquiring speech, through trauma or disease.
- Adults with serious hearing loss who are not benefiting from hearing aids.

How the Implant Works

The cochlear implant takes over the function of the inner ear. The implantable portion includes an electronic receiver, the electrode array, and wire. A small surgical incision is made, and the receiver is placed in the skull behind the ear. Attached to the receiver is the wire with the electrode array, which is inserted into the cochlea.

The remaining portions of the cochlear implant are all on the outside. These include a microphone, receiver, speech processor, and a magnetic link between the outer scalp and the implanted portion of the device. The microphone attaches to the speech processor by a thin cord. The processor is worn either in a pocket or on a belt around the waist and is powered by batteries. The processor is a powerful mini-computer that filters, analyzes, and digitizes sounds into coded signals. The signals are then sent through a thin transmitting coil to the cochlear implant under the skin. The implant then sends the electrical energy to the electrodes in the cochlea to stimulate the nerve fibers. The electrical sound is then sent to the brain for processing.

FACT

Heather Whitestone McCallum, Miss America of 1995, received a cochlear implant in August 2002. Since the implant, she has already heard a variety of sounds, such as water running from a faucet, a van door opening, and the sound of hair spray coming out of the bottle. It will take Heather anywhere from three to five years to learn how to interpret the more complex sounds of speech and music.

This entire time lapse between what the person hears and what the brain processes is microseconds. (The surgery takes approximately two to four hours and generally requires an overnight hospital stay.) Presently, scientists are developing smaller, faster, and enhanced speech processors. This will improve the perception of speech and music. During the next three to five years, the goal of the scientists is to also make these devices fully implantable. Since 1972, 70,000 people worldwide have received cochlear implants.

The Cochlear Implant Education Center

In the United States, as of 2002, there have been approximately 21,000 implants. On the campus of Gallaudet University, there has been a recent addition, the Cochlear Implant Education Center. This center is located in the Laurent Clerc National Deaf Education Center.

ESSENTIAL

The medical world is working to bring about many changes and improvements for the health and care of our future populations. Nonetheless, the Rubella Bulge population will be getting older, and these people will have their share of medical issues. The medical community will find itself in need of many more people with a knowledge of sign language.

The Cochlear Implant Education Center does not provide cochlear implant surgical services. Its function is to investigate and evaluate cochlear implant technology and its role in the lives of deaf children, from birth to high school. Cochlear implants have been very controversial. Parents need to investigate all information put forth regarding these implants before making any decisions.

Additional Resources

If you are interested in additional information regarding cochlear implants, you'll find a range of options available.

Web Sites
- *www.clerccenter.gallaudet.edu*
- *www.earsurgery.org/cochlear*

Books
- *The Parent's Guide to Cochlear Implants* by Patricia M. Chute and Mary Ellen Nevins
- *Cochlear Implants in Children* by John B. Christiansen and Irene W. Leigh
- *The Handbook of Pediatric Audiology* by Sanford E. Gerber
- *The Handbook of Cochlear Implants and Children* by Nancy Tye-Murray
- *Cochlear Implants: A Handbook* by Bonnie Poitras Tucker
- *Children with Cochlear Implants in Educational Settings* by Mary Ellen Nevins and Patricia M. Chute
- *Hear Again Back to Life* by Arlene Romoff

Movies
- *Sound and Fury*
- *Twins*
- *Cochlear Implants: Covering the Basics*

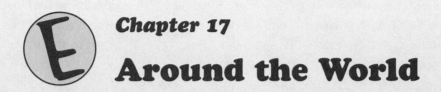

Chapter 17

Around the World

Everyone loves to plan that special get-away-from-it-all vacation. Traveling and seeing new places is always exciting. Whether you are planning a vacation, or whether you work in travel and tourism, this chapter offers interesting information, such as ADA mandates as they relate to hotels, regional variations in signs, travel directions, and related signs.

Sign Variations

Often, people wonder if signs are the same all across the United States. The answer is no. There are regional sign variations. These variations can be seen in the formation, placement, or direction of the signs. Nearly all large cities have variations in proper name signs. They also have fingerspelled abbreviations that are specific to the geographical area. For the most part, it is quite easy to adapt to these small and sometimes subtle sign differences. The variations can be compared to the various accents that we hear across the United States.

> There are fun sign language books available that show you many of the sign variations. You will find some of them listed in Appendix B.

The variations in signs require signers to be flexible. Staying flexible is one of the important traits that will aid you in your journey to become a terrific signer. Keep in mind that the best signer is not necessarily the one who has the biggest sign vocabulary. The best signer is the one who knows how to *use* the vocabulary he or she has acquired.

While you are learning sign language, keep in mind the following list of positive traits that will help to make you a well-rounded signer. A good signer will do the following:

- Know more than one way to sign a word.
- Be flexible in acquiring signed vocabulary.
- Be flexible in applying sign.
- Respect regional variations.
- Inquire about variations in regional signs.

On the Road Again

Have you ever wanted to be a world traveler? Now you can! Well, at least you can make a mental journey during this sign language lesson. We'll start here in America and then travel to foreign countries.

Around the World

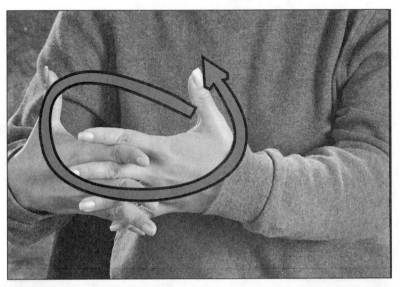

▲ **AMERICA:** To sign "America," hold all the fingers on both hands in an interlocked position, and rotate. The hand position can also be vertical

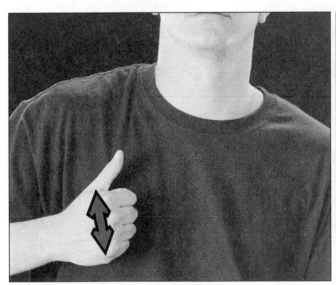

▲ **CANADA:** To sign "Canada," use the "A" hand and grasp and shake the lapel, imitating shaking the snow off a coat.

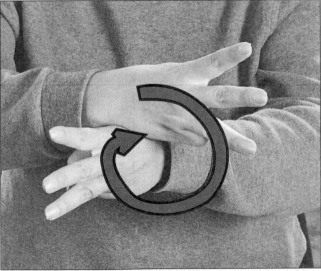

▲ **WORLD:** To sign "world," simultaneously rotate the "W" hands around each other once.

Around the World

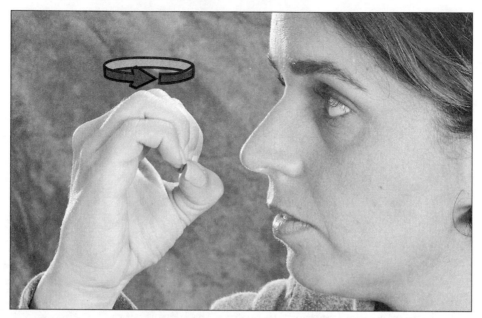

▲ **EUROPE:** To sign "Europe," circle the "E" hand in front of the face.

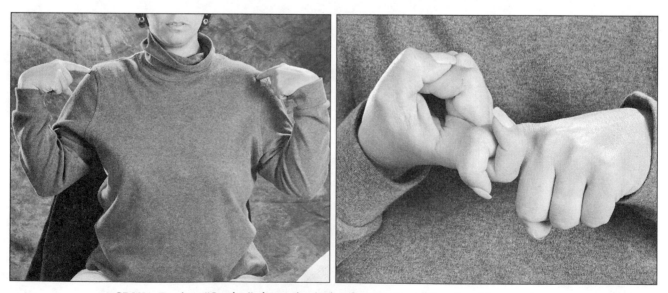

▲ **SPAIN:** To sign "Spain," draw the index fingers from the shoulders and hook them together, imitating tying a large scarf.

Around the World

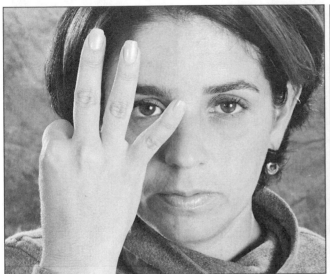

▲ **FRANCE:** To sign "France," turn the "F" hand outward to face the reader.

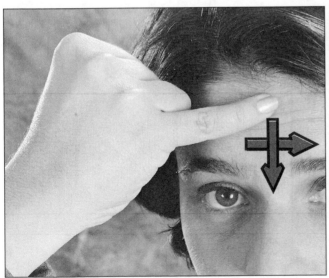

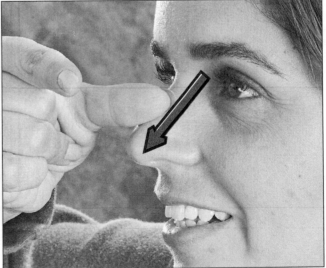

▲ **ITALY:** To sign "Italy," use the "I" hand to draw a cross in the middle of the forehead.

▲ **GREECE:** To sign "Greece," draw the "G" hand down the nose.

Around the World

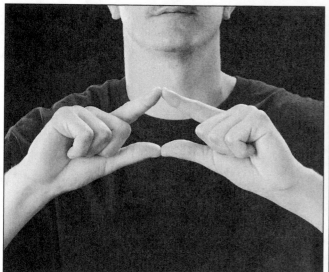
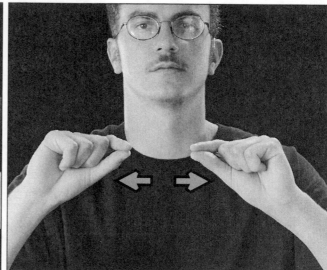

▲ **JAPAN:** To sign "Japan," touch the fingertips of the "G" hand at the neck, then pull them apart.

Cars, Trucks, Trains, and Planes

▲ **CAR, DRIVE:** To sign "car" or "drive," use the "S" hands, imitating holding a steering wheel.

▲ **MOTORCYCLE:** To sign "motorcycle," the downturned "S" hands imitate driving a motorcycle.

Cars, Trucks, Trains, and Planes

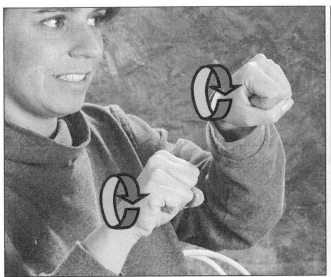

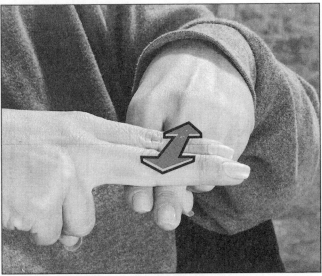

▲ **BICYCLE:** To sign "bicycle," rotate the "S" hands, imitating a peddling motion.

▲ **TRAIN:** To sign "train," rub the right "H" hand back and forth on top of the left "H" hand, imitating railroad tracks.

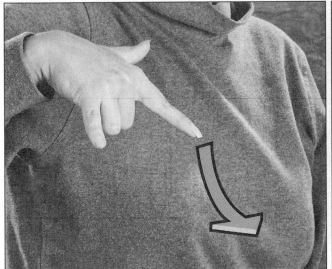

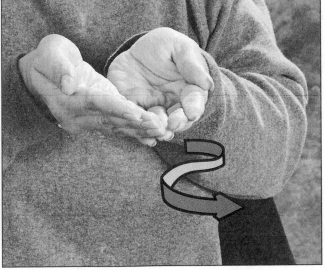

▲ **AIRPLANE, JET, FLY:** To sign "airplane," "jet," or "fly," move the hand forward with the thumb, index, and pinky fingers extended, imitating a flying airplane with bouncy movement for nouns, steady movement for verbs.

▲ **BOAT:** To sign "boat," move the hands forward, back, and forth as if going through water.

In addition, it is important to know how to use the "three-finger" classifier. This classifier allows you to show the movement or location of the mode of transportation you are describing.

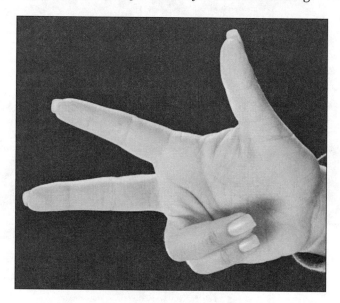

◀ The three-finger classifier is made with the thumb up and the index and middle finger extended.

Once you form this handshape, you can move it in all directions. Think of it as your mini-car (or plane or whatever vehicle you choose). This handshape indicates movement, and it assists you when used in describing your travels. For instance, you can use this handshape to describe one car cutting off another. Use both hands, each representing a car, and simply show the movement of each.

Location and Direction

Signing directions are easy. Now that you know your ABCs, here is another chance to apply them. When giving directions to go north, south, east, or west, you will use initialized signs. Sign these four directions:

1. North is indicated by moving the "N" hand straight up, skyward.
2. South is indicated by moving the "S" hand straight downward.
3. East is indicated by moving the "E" hand horizontally to the right.
4. West is indicated by moving the "W" hand horizontally to the left.

While giving or receiving directions, it is always good to know when you are going up, down, right, or left. Sign the directions for these four signs:

1. Right is indicated by moving the "R" hand horizontally to the right.
2. Left is indicated by moving the "L" hand horizontally to the left.
3. Up is indicated by the extended index finger pointing and moving upward.
4. Down is indicated by the extended index finger pointing downward.

Time for a Vacation

Deaf people enjoy vacations the same as everyone else. However, they have justified concerns when staying at hotels. They need wake-up calls, visual smoke detectors, doorbells, and phones. Thanks to the ADA, the federal legislation that ensures hotels accommodate deaf and hard of hearing patrons, the stress related to vacations is seriously reduced. According to the ADA, the hotel shall provide the following accommodations for these patrons:

- Visual alarm clock
- Visual smoke alarm
- Telephone signalers
- TTYs
- Closed-caption decoders
- Doorbell notification

Thanks to these mandates, the deaf and hard of hearing no longer need to hand-carry their own visual signaling devices onto airplanes when they are traveling. Given the current status of baggage screening of luggage at airports, the ability of the deaf to travel lightly relieves a lot of stress and is very welcome.

Sign language on a resume is a wonderful enhancer. This is especially true when applying for a position as a service provider or a position that provides public services.

As discussed in Chapter 1, the need to provide services for the deaf and hard of hearing increases yearly. If your line of work is in hotel, travel, or tourism, your ability to use sign language will make everyone's travel experience pleasurable. To start you off in this area of signed vocabulary, here are five commonly used signs.

▲ **VACATION, HOLIDAY:** To sign "vacation" or "holiday," place the thumbs of the "open five" hands at the armpits then wiggle the fingers.

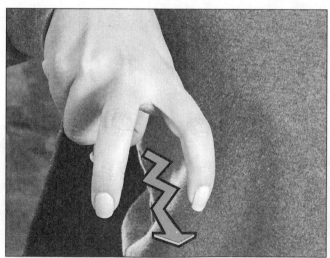

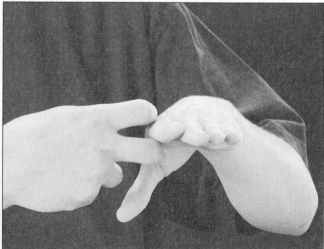

▲ **TRAVEL:** To sign "travel," extend the slightly curved index and middle finger downward and move forward in a zigzag fashion.

▲ **TICKETS:** To sign "tickets," the "bent V" hand grasps the flat left hand, imitating punching the ticket.

Time for a Vacation

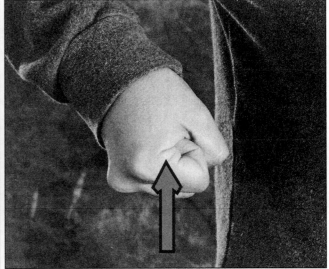

▲ **VISIT:** To sign "visit," the "V" hands are rotated alternately, imitating people traveling. Rotating the "Vs" toward you indicates people visiting you; rotating the "Vs" away from you indicates that you are traveling.

▲ **SUITCASE:** To sign "suitcase," imitate lifting the handle of the suitcase. A variation for the new style of luggage is to pull a handle, imitating a suitcase with wheels.

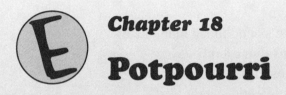

Chapter 18

Potpourri

In this chapter, you'll find a variety of things. We're going to take a look at a couple of new methods of communication just to give you an idea of what's out there. You're also going to find out just how much you've learned and discover a few new signs.

Finding Out How Much You Know

We are drawing very close to the end of our lessons, and it's time for a pop quiz. Let's see how much you remember. You made it this far, so you can do this. Ready? Here is your list of questions. (No peeking at the answers!)

1. What is an iconic sign?
2. How do you become skilled in sign language?
3. Is sign language the same everywhere?
4. How do you ask questions?
5. How are differences in gender indicated?
6. What is the signing space?
7. What is a sign?
8. How do I make a sign for someone's name?
9. How do you indicate past, present, and future?
10. What is the Deaf community?

How do you think you did? You'll soon find out. Here are the answers.

1. An iconic sign closely resembles what it represents.
2. You become skilled in sign language with practice, practice, practice.
3. Sign language differs from region to region and around the world.
4. You ask questions by leaning forward with a quizzical facial expression and eyebrows down.
5. Gender is indicated by the placement and location of the sign: forehead for male, jaw line for female.
6. Signing space is where most of the signs are formed. It encompasses the area from the top of the head to the waist.
7. A sign is a unit of language that is formed with distinctive handshapes, locations, specific movements, and facial expressions.
8. People's names may be fingerspelled, or they may have a unique name sign.
9. Past is indicated by a backward movement. Present is formed directly in front of the body. Future is a forward movement from the body.
10. The Deaf community is a cultural group of people who share common values, language, and experiences.

Everyday Chatter

The following shows some common expressions used in everyday chatter. Some of these you've already learned, but it's always good to refresh your memory. You'll be able to use these words several times a day, so take advantage of each and every chance you have to practice your new skills on others.

▲ **HELLO, GOODBYE:** To sign "hello" or "goodbye," wave the "flat" hand.

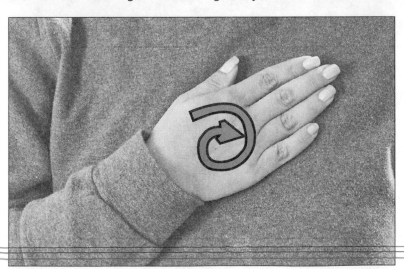

▲ **PLEASE:** To sign "please," circle the "flat" hand on the chest.

Everyday Chatter

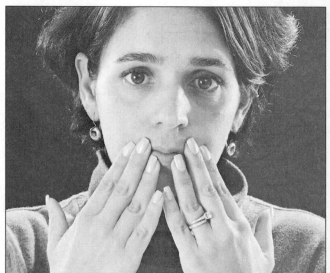

▲ **THANK YOU:** To sign "thank you," place the fingertips of the "open" palms on the chin, then bring them down, palms facing up.

▲ **NO:** To sign "no," bring the extended thumb, index, and middle fingers together.

Everyday Chatter

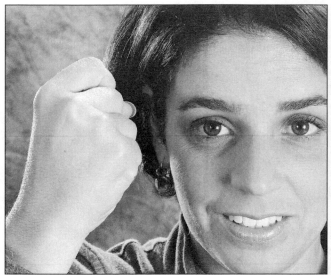

▲ **UNDERSTAND:** To sign "understand," make a fist at the temple, then snap open the index finger to a vertical position.

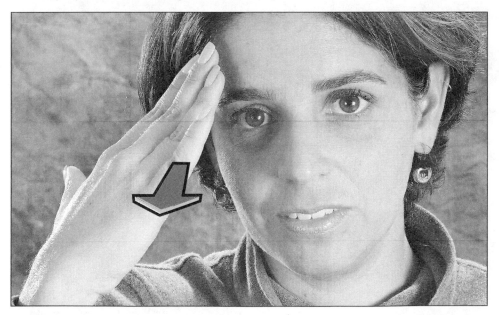

▲ **KNOW, KNOWLEDGE:** To sign "know" or "knowledge," place the flat hand at the temple.

Using Games to Learn

Games are a great way to practice fingerspelling and signed vocabulary while having fun and learning. We will use signs and subjects that we talk about daily. The games presented here are simple sign language games for beginners, with easy-to-follow instructions. Teachers, child care providers, parents, adults, and children alike can all share in the fun.

The first game is the chain name game. The first player fingerspells his name. The second player fingerspells the first player's name and adds his own. The game continues around the room until it comes back to the first person, who spells the entire group's names.

The next game asks you to fingerspell by touch. One player fingerspells, while the other player, with eyes closed, tries to read the word by the feel of the handshape against their hand. Fingerspelling by touch is challenging, yet at the same time it is very interesting. In order to enjoy this game at its fullest, begin by fingerspelling three-letter words. When you have mastered the list of three-letter words, move on to words of four letters, then five, and so on.

Here is another fun game to test your signing comprehension. One player signs food and cooking items, while the other players write the signed words out. It is easier to form the signs than it is to read the signs. This game will provide you with a way to have fun and practice at the same time.

This next game puts your number acquisition to the test. Exchange the following information using fingerspelling and numbers: age; shoe size; license plate number; cell, work, and home phone numbers; family members' ages; and zip code.

This game presents you with a challenge of applying facial and body language. One player acts out a function of a household object, and the other players guess the item. Examples: cutting meat equals "knife"; washing hands equals "soap"; unlocking door equals "key"; and sleeping equals "bed."

For the next game, one player fingerspells a clue, and the other players must guess the sport. Examples: "tee" equals "golf" and "bow" equals "archery." You can apply variations to this game by changing the groups to household items, office supplies, or things that are associated with recreation, places, and movies.

Try each one of these games. You are sure to find a favorite. The best kind of learning is the kind that is enjoyable.

Magic Wand Game

The goal of the magic wand game is to facilitate and increase the use of facial expressions, body language, and pantomime. As you develop your signing skills and learn to apply classifiers, this list will be useful to you. Nevertheless, until then, you will be able to simply use them just like a game of charades.

Use an imaginary wand whose dimensions are described with the use of classifiers and mime. Players may sign additional information to give more clues while describing the item. Sign the following items using the imaginary wand and facial expressions, body language, or pantomime to describe the item.

conductor's baton	baseball bat	hammer
screwdriver	thermometer	rolling pin
pencil	cane	paintbrush
ruler	straw	pogo stick
golf club	umbrella	mop/broom
cigarette	toilet brush	flagpole
drumstick	lipstick	toothpick
violin bow	nail file	stick of gum
spoon	sewing needle	crowbar
telescope	meat thermometer	jackhammer
pipe	toilet tissue holder	garden hose

(continued) ▶

knitting needle	belt	letter opener
crochet hook	window shade	curling wand
flute	bicycle pump	oil/transmission stick
bubble wand	toothbrush	bathroom towel bar
fishing pole	curtain rod	empty paper towel tube
plunger	can of room spray	yoke for carrying buckets
mascara	turkey baster	weed trimmer
computer mouse	tennis racket	telephone pole
washing machine	umbrella	cookie tin
remote control	candle	ironing board

Now that you have tried gesturing and miming the magic wand items, you need to try practicing a few of them applying classifiers. The next time you use this chart, visualize each item, then shape each item using the classifiers. The classifiers make it easier to describe things that are cylindrical, flat, thin, or vertical, as we discussed in Chapter 7.

Total Communication

Total Communication (or TC) emphasizes the use of all methods of communicating. The benefit of TC is that it opens all the doors, using every practical mode to teach vocabulary and language. The final goal is to communicate using any, and all, methods with the deaf and hard of hearing and perhaps the special needs child.

The following is a list of some of the methods used in TC:

- American Sign Language
- Signed Exact English
- Contact Sign Language/Pidgin Sign English
- Fingerspelling
- Lip reading
- Body language

- Facial expressions
- Oral speech
- Simultaneous communication, or sim-com (speech and signs used at the same time)
- Auditory/Verbal
- Cued speech (see below)
- Amplification devices
- Writing
- Drawing
- Pantomime

Cued Speech

In 1966, Doctor R. Orin Cornett at Gallaudet University developed cued speech. This visual communication system has been adapted for more than fifty languages. Cued speech is a method whereby the speaker adds eight handshapes in four different locations to distinguish between similar sounds. This adds clarity to the spoken language by identifying each distinctive speech sound. It is used for phonic instruction, articulation therapy, and for individuals, regardless of the etiology, who have difficulty with speech. Some late-deafened adults rely on the assistance of cued speech for lip reading and maintaining their functional speech control. Ⓔ

Chapter 19

Expressing Yourself with Signing

Learning to sign a song can be one of the most satisfying challenges for the novice signer. You'll also find that dancing and signing can be combined to create an exciting visual. Combining sign language with all its facial expressions and body language adds emphasis to a stage performance and easily translates to an audience. Get ready to take a bow.

Signing Music

Signed music is visually enchanting. It is also a great way to practice sign language. Adults quickly learn to enjoy signing music, and it is good exercise too. Children learn to love it because it's fun, and, at the same time, it improves their motor skills. In addition, signing the words to a song enhances memory skills for young and old alike. Once a child or adult signs a song, he or she easily remembers the lyrics and rarely forgets them.

On May 7, 1824, Ludwig van Beethoven's Ninth Symphony was performed in Vienna. Beethoven, at this time, was completely deaf and could not conduct the premiere. He did, however, stand next to the conductor. At the end of the performance, he remained unaware of the applause of the emotional audience until a soloist had him turn to face them.

When you approach the idea of signing music, it is best to do first things first. The first thing you need to do is select an appropriate song for your maiden voyage. You will play and sign your song many, many times before you satisfactorily sign it, so consider choosing a song that you enjoy hearing each time it plays. It is best if you select one for which you already know the lyrics. You don't want to learn how to form new signs and try to memorize new lyrics at the same time. The lyrics should be simple with clear meanings. Conceptual songs are difficult to translate from English to sign language, and for the novice signer, this is not always an easy task. So it is a good idea to keep it simple.

Your song should not be excessively slow or fast, as these types of tempos require a high level of control while moving the signs to the music. Also, try to select a song that has repeating lyrics. The repetition will assist you in controlling the signs and, at the same time, build your rhythm. To wrap it all up for you in one statement: select a song you enjoy, one with simple lyrics you know, and one that has a moderate tempo. Place these considerations at the top of your list, and you will be well on your way to signing a good song.

Translating to Signs

Once you've chosen a song, you'll then need to look at the lyrics carefully and begin the process of translating them from English to signs.

- Write down all the lyrics, line by line.
- Omit all the small words, such as "a," "the," "is," and "an."
- Write the approximate sign equivalents of the words or concepts of the lyrics.

Go with the Flow

The translation of a song may require a few attempts before it is just right. Once you have mastered the appropriate signs, you can begin to connect them with the rhythm of the song. The time you put into this mode of signing will really show. Here are six helpful tips:

1. When translating the lyrics from English to signs, always think of what the lyrics are really trying to convey.
2. When practicing, sign your song three times in a row, take a break, and start over again.
3. Feet should be slightly apart, never together, thereby giving you the ability to flex and flow with the music.
4. Always use appropriate facial expressions and body language that matches the lyrics.
5. Never drop your hands to your sides while signing your song. Doing so stops the music visually.
6. Sign your song with the music, never without.

Don't be discouraged if you cannot fully sign your song in the first few attempts. Practice your song repeatedly, and you will get there. The time you put into it will give you the desired results. Try to make the learning process and the practice all part of the fun of signing a song.

Phyllis Frelich won the Tony Award for Best Actress in the Broadway play *Children of a Lesser God*. Miss Frelich is profoundly deaf. In 1991, she also became the first deaf person to be elected to the Screen Actors Guild Board in Hollywood.

Practicing and learning new signs for music builds confidence in your new signing abilities. The simplicity of learning to sign a song will also stimulate you, perhaps without realizing it, into applying many of the basic principles of ASL. These principles range from translating English to signs, applying facial expressions, and using body language.

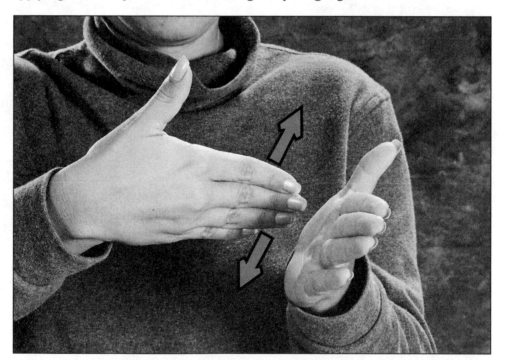

▲ **MUSIC, SONG:** To sign "music" or "song," wave the "flat" hand onto the left palm and arm.

Visual Tapestries Within the Arts

Blending sign language and music often touches and emotionally moves audiences with its beauty. Combining dance with sign language also creates a visual delight. It adds a wonderful extension to a dance performance. The same is true of a stage performance that has been extended with manual signs and strong facial expressions. A signed song can be likened to creating an enchanting visual tapestry, a tapestry on which graceful signs with pleasant facials and body language are all woven together, to bring music to visual life. These visual tapestries within the arts are delightful, enjoyable, and appreciated by young and old, signing and nonsigning alike.

Heart and Soul

Religious hymns and songs expressed with the added element of sign language are powerful. They seem to help lift one's faith. The signs for heaven, soul, and angel are remarkably beautiful.

▲ **HEAVEN:** To sign "heaven," place palms facing each other with hands vertical, then cross hands and arms above the head in an arched movement and spread arms open.

▲ **SOUL:** To sign "soul," pull the "F" hand upward in a spiral movement rising out of the left "C" hand.

Heart and Soul

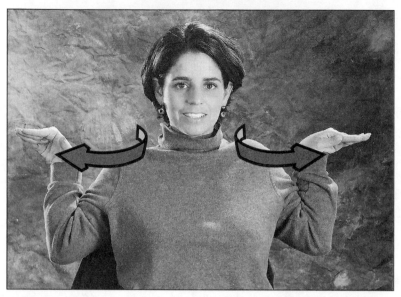

▲ **ANGEL:** To sign "angel," place fingertips of both hands on the shoulders, then twist forward and out off the shoulders, imitating wings.

Developing Facial Expressions and Body Language

Let's try a visualization exercise. This type of exercise is like a game of charades and works toward developing facial expressions and body language. The following signs have been previously shown to you in earlier chapters. But now you're going to sign while adding the elements of facial and body language. This time, there are no photo illustrations to guide you. Instead, you will find only the word, followed by the appropriate facial expression and body language.

As you know, facial expressions and body language are very important parts of sign language. Remember, they add an element of clarity and comprehension. The following chart will assist you in developing and enhancing these important elements. You will need to take a moment to look at the word and visualize what you see.

Sign/Word	Facial Expression	Body Language
Crazy	Rolling eyes, tongue out	Side-to-side head movement
Dentist	Wide-eyed	Head back, mouth open, tense body
Dictionary	Eyes down, looking studious	Turn slightly left from the waist up
Flower	Bright-eyed and pleased	Smell the fragrance, head tilts, shoulders up
Happy	Large, bright-eyed smile	Loose and relaxed neck and head
Lion	Fierce look, furrowed brows, focused eyes	Proud, powerful posture
Mirror	Admiring look	Head tilts side to side, chin up slightly
Motorcycle	Determined	Body forward, head down slightly, hands gripped
Napkin	Proper look, lips tightly together	Chin up, head tilted back slightly
Proud	Smiling, smug look, lips together	Shoulders back, chest out, chin up
Strawberry	Lips pursed as in kissing	Chin up, right shoulder rolls

Building all the required elements into your signing requires some talent in the area of multitasking. Don't become frustrated at the beginning if you can't do it all. Instead, slowly learn to take on the character and posture of what it is you are trying to express or convey. Simply explained, you need to have a smile when you sign "happy," not to wear a frown. The same is true in reverse. If you are signing "angry," show the appropriate facial. Start slowly, and practice the facial and body language described in the chart. Continue until you become comfortable with these postures. Before you even realize it, adding the appropriate facial expressions and body language will become second nature.

Chapter 20

New Age of
Sign Language

Using sign language with babies is a great way to get your baby started into language acquisition. Today, research is proving that teaching simple baby signs to your infant assists their development and raises IQ scores. In this chapter, you will learn to form the recommended first signs for babies. In addition, there is a healthy hearing baby checklist.

Baby Talk

Babies understand signs and are able to sign before they know how to talk. The reason for this is simple. Babies are able to manipulate their little hands long before they can manipulate their mouths to articulate words. Surely you've seen a baby respond to the gestural language of a pair of outstretched arms and the facial expression of a big smile.

Benefits of Sign Communication

Early sign communication with babies produces significant benefits, including the following:

- Presents building blocks to self-esteem.
- Reduces frustration.
- Improves communication.
- Stimulates language acquisition.
- Enhances intellectual development.

Recommended Baby Signs

Signing with baby is fun and enjoyable. It also will strengthen the parent-to-infant bond. Begin signing from the age of four to six months, when baby's focusing skills develops. Start out simply with just one or two signs, such as milk and mommy. Reinforce these signs by signing them repeatedly. This repetition allows the baby to start to make the connection between the signs and the objects. Continue to build vocabulary with your baby daily. At eight to nine months of age, expect to see your baby start to sign back. Of course, this time is variable; infants develop at their own rate. It is important to remember that signing with your baby encourages speech development.

Begin your baby signs with this recommended list.

Baby Signs

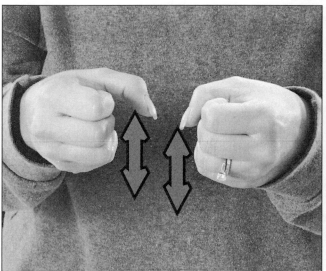

▲ **MILK:** To sign "milk," squeeze both "S" hands alternately up and down, imitating milking a cow. This sign may also be formed using just one hand.

▲ **BABY:** To sign "baby," cradle an imaginary baby in your arms, then rock.

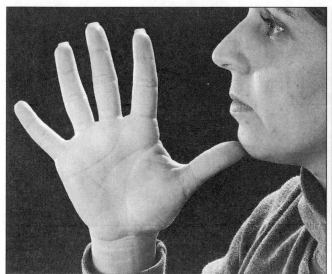

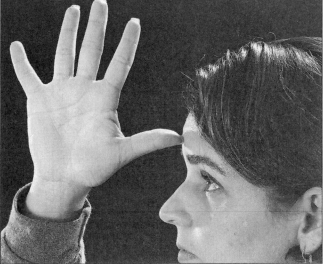

▲ **MOMMY:** To sign "mommy," use an "open five" hand, and place the tip of the thumb on the chin, palm facing left. Either wiggle all the fingers in the "open five" hand, or tap the thumb of the "open five" hand on the chin repeatedly.

▲ **DADDY:** To sign "daddy," use an "open five" hand, and place the tip of the thumb on the forehead, palm facing left. Either wiggle all the fingers in the "open five" hand, or tap the thumb of the "open five" hand on the forehead repeatedly.

Baby Signs

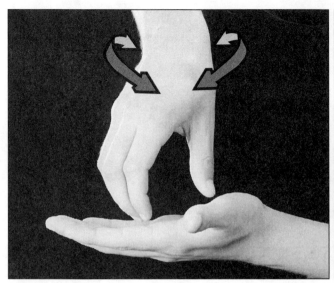

▲ **COOKIE:** To sign "cookie," place the fingertips of the "C" hand onto the left palm, then twist as if cutting out cookies.

▲ **WANT, DESIRE:** To sign "want" or "desire," pull both curved "five" hands toward the body.

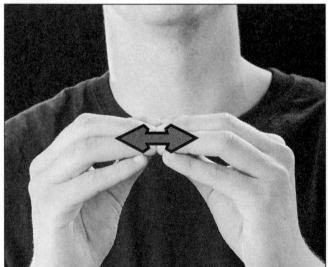

▲ **MORE:** To sign "more," tap the fingers of both flat "O" hands together.

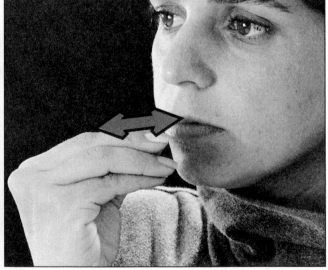

▲ **EAT:** To sign "eat," move the flat "O" hand toward mouth, lightly tap the lips, imitating eating.

Baby Signs

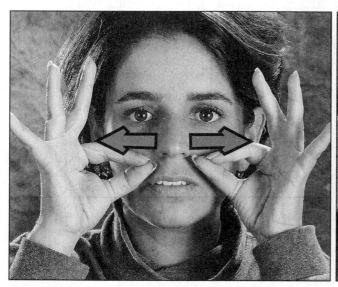

▲ **CAT:** To sign "cat," move the "F" hands from each side of the mouth, drawing out to the sides, representing the cat's whiskers.

▲ **ANIMAL:** To sign "animal," place the fingertips of both hands on the chest and rock the hands back and forth, imitating an animal breathing.

It is exciting to sign with babies during the formative first two years of life. It is wonderful to know that by signing with your baby, you are enhancing language and speech formation. Remember, sign consistently with your baby. Keep a journal of your baby's sign language progress, and include a few photos of baby signing. Someday, that journal might become a very special keepsake.

FACT

In newborns, the incidence of severe to profound hearing loss occurs in anywhere from five to thirty babies out of every 10,000 born. Later in this chapter, you will be provided with a list of signs that indicate healthy hearing in your child.

Perhaps you have introduced baby signs into your child's world during the first two formative years and have been pleased with the results. But now you're faced with selecting a child care center. Don't be afraid to ask the child care staff if sign language is a part of their playing and learning. Today, many early child care providers are attending sign language classes and in-services. The goal of the child care provider who has taken sign language is to apply sign in the daily activities of the children and to continue to enhance language and build cognitive skills.

Hearing Health

As you are working on language development, it is advisable to ensure that your baby has normal hearing and that your little one continues to stay healthy. To help you with this, the following sections provide hearing health checklists for babies according to age.

Birth to Three Months
- Responds to sounds with blinks, or may be startled.
- Attentive when hearing an unfamiliar noise or being called.
- Awakens at loud sounds.
- Responds to parents' voices.
- Creates cooing noises.
- Responds to noisy stimuli in the environment.

Four to Five Months
- Responds to sounds by turning the head and eyes.

Six to Nine Months
- Responds to nearly all environmental sounds.
- Looks in the appropriate direction of sounds.

Nine to Twelve Months
- Begins to imitate simple words.
- Begins to use voice to get attention.

Be cautious with your baby's hearing by always maintaining a hearing health safeguard. The purpose of this safeguard is simply to keep loud damaging noises from entering into your baby's surroundings.

Simplified Signs

Simplified signs are signs that have been modified and are used in an adaptive manner for special populations. These populations might include special needs students or those with physical challenges and language limitations. The tendency when modifying signs is to simplify the formation of the sign itself. This simplification creates an ease of movement for those with limitations. In addition, these signs are often more iconic, made to closely resemble the word that is being signed.

QUESTION?

What is an iconic sign?
An iconic sign is a pictorial representation. The formation, shape, and/or movement of an iconic sign can closely represent the visual imagery of the word.

Various programs have adopted the use of adaptive signs successfully. Keep in mind that these modified, simplified signs are not part of the pure ASL. However, signs that have been adapted to serve specific populations truly have a positive impact and effect. Often, when these particular populations are given sign language as a means of enhancing communication, it decreases the frustration felt by these individuals. Generally, these modified, simplified signs are single vocabulary words and are used and applied in a manner similar to the home signs discussed in Chapter 1.

Many Faces of Sign

As you've learned, there are many wonderful applications for sign language, and these applications extend beyond the Deaf community. An interest in this mode of communication is on the rise. However, this interest creates some concern within the Deaf community for their beloved language. Often, they express that changes, modifications, simplifications, and misuse all have the potential to corrupt the pure ASL. But all languages evolve and change over time. A language has to be flexible enough to bring in the new and do away with the old.

During the average year, a member of the Deaf community, a native signer, or an interpreter will come up with the need for a new sign purely out of necessity. A good example of a new sign is the one that applies to the ever-changing world of technology, "e-mail." Of course, there will be regional variations on new signs. Newly created signs that prove to be useful, easy to form, and are quickly recognizable will be the signs that are accepted by the Deaf community. As the saying goes: "Necessity is the mother of invention."

Now that you have achieved a fundamental understanding of sign language, perhaps you will continue your learning and join the many faces of sign. Maybe you will be the new face in an ASL classroom or Deaf community. Signers are all around you. They are educators, medical personnel, and a broad spectrum of service providers, and their numbers are growing. There is no limit to the uses of sign language, and your education does not have to end when you close this book. Your personal motivation will guide you to find opportunities to practice and use signs. Search local communities for resources that can help you reach a greater proficiency of American Sign Language and build your confidence. Best of luck in your journey!

Appendices

Appendix A
Quizzes and Games

Appendix B
Resources

Appendix C
Glossary

Appendix A

Quizzes and Games

Alphabet Quiz

Read each question and fill in the blank with the
appropriate letter from the Manual Alphabet.

1. To form the letter -------------, cross
the index finger and the middle finger.
All other fingers are tightly tucked away.

2. To form the letter -------------, all
fingers are vertical with the thumb in the
palm.

3. To form the letter -------------, make
a fist and hold the pinky finger in the
vertical position.

4. To form the letter -------------, place
the thumb between the index finger and
the middle finger. Tuck the last two fingers
into the palm and out of the way. Drop
your wrist so the middle finger and index
fingers are inverted and facing downward.

5. To form the letter -------------, tuck the
thumb between the index finger and the
middle finger.

6. To form the letter -------------, extend
the thumb and the pinky finger with all
other fingers tucked against the palm of the
hand.

7. To form the letter -------------, place all
fingers on the thumb, except for the index
finger, which should be in an upright,
vertical position.

8. To form the letter -------------, place
the thumb between the index finger and
the middle finger. Hold in an upright
vertical position. The last two fingers should
be tucked away into the palm and out of
the way.

9. To form the letter -------------, pinch
the index finger to the thumb. The last
three fingers are in a semi-vertical position.

10. To form the letter -------------, swing
the forefinger and middle finger horizontally
to the left with the thumb down and tucked
away.

True/False Awareness Quiz

Read each question and circle the appropriate answer.

True or **False**   **1.** The first school for the deaf was established in 1817 in Hartford, Connecticut.

True or **False**   **2.** The uppercase word "Deaf" refers to the Deaf community, which shares a common language, cultural heritage, and similar interest.

True or **False**   **3.** American Sign Language, known as ASL, is the natural native language of the American Deaf Community.

True or **False**   **4.** Genders are indicated by forming male signs near the forehead and female signs on the chin or jaw line.

True or **False**   **5.** The Deaf community is a group of Deaf people who share common values, language, and experiences.

True or **False**   **6.** Maintaining eye contact at all times with the signer is extremely important.

True or **False**   **7.** Signs are formed the same way whether you are right or left-handed.

True or **False**   **8.** A gesture is an expressive body movement that can convey an idea, feeling, or concept.

True or **False**   **9.** An interpreter is a person who facilitates communication between the deaf, hard of hearing, and hearing persons by translating spoken language into sign and vice versa.

True or **False**   **10.** The manual alphabet represents the thirty-six letters of the English alphabet.

Letter Form Quiz

Read each question and circle the appropriate answers.

1. Circle the seven letters of the alphabet that are formed with a closed hand.

A B C D E F G H I J K L M
N O P Q R S T U V W X Y Z

2. Circle the twelve letters of the alphabet that are formed in a vertical position.

A B C D E F G H I J K L M
N O P Q R S T U V W X Y Z

3. Circle the two letters of the alphabet that are formed in a horizontal position.

A B C D E F G H I J K L M
N O P Q R S T U V W X Y Z

4. Circle the two letters of the alphabet that are formed open, inverted, and downward.

A B C D E F G H I J K L M
N O P Q R S T U V W X Y Z

Sign Practice Quiz

Read each question and fill in the blank with the appropriate word.

1. To sign "_____," place your palm on your chest.

2. To sign "_____," cross and tap the "H" hands twice.

3. To sign "_____," clap hands twice.

4. To sign "_____," stroke the "flat" hand on the left "open" palm several times.

5. To sign "_____," raise both hands high in the air in an "open five" position and shake them.

6. To sign "_____," draw the "T" hand down the cheek.

7. To sign "_____," squeeze both "S" hands alternately up and down.

8. To sign "_____," place the fingertips of the "open" palms on the chin, then bring down the palms facing up.

Sign Practice Quiz (continued)

9. To sign "------------------------------," place all the fingertips into the left palm. Next, pull upward with a modified "O" hand and place it on the forehead.

10. To sign "------------------------------," place the "B" hand to the chin, then bring the "B" hand down and place it in the left palm.

11. To sign "------------------------------," use the "flat" hand, move it forward and down.

12. To sign "------------------------------," move "flat" hands forward, palms facing each other.

13. To sign "------------------------------," use a closed hand starting at the chin, open to "flat" hand while circling the face.

14. To sign "------------------------------," use the "flat" hand, palm facing back, and push it over the shoulder.

15. To sign "------------------------------," touch the tips of both "I" hands and pull them apart in a circular motion.

16. To sign "------------------------------," place the index and middle fingertips into the left "open" palm.

17. To sign "------------------------------," circle the "flat" hand on the chest.

18. To sign "------------------------------," place the fingertips of both hands on the chest and rock back and forth.

19. To sign "------------------------------," use both "flat" hands, palms facing each other, and move hands straight down.

20. To sign "------------------------------," place the "flat" hand at the temple.

21. To sign "------------------------------," place the "S" hand at the temple and then snap open the index finger.

22. To sign "------------------------------," move the "F" hands from each side of the mouth outward.

23. To sign "------------------------------," twist "F" hands alternately back and forth several times, then add "person."

24. To sign "------------------------------," rub the right "H" back and forth on top of the left "H" hand.

25. To sign "------------------------------," use the "S" hands, closed fists facing up, and open hands quickly many times.

Quiz Answers

Alphabet Quiz Answers

1. R
2. B
3. I
4. P
5. T
6. Y
7. D
8. K
9. F
10. H

True/False Awareness Quiz Answers

Questions 1 through 9 are all True.
Question 10 is False—there are twenty-six letters in the English alphabet. Just checking to see if you were snoozing!

Letter Form Quiz Answers

1. A E O M N S T are formed with a closed hand.
2. B D F I K L R U V W X Y are formed in a vertical position.
3. G H are formed in a horizontal position.
4. P Q are formed open, inverted, and downward.

Sign Practice Quiz Answers

1. My, mine
2. Name
3. School
4. Excuse
5. Applause
6. Tan
7. Milk
8. Thank you
9. Learn
10. Good
11. Future
12. Road
13. Beautiful
14. Past
15. Spaghetti
16. Stand
17. Please
18. Animal
19. Person
20. Know
21. Understand
22. Cat
23. Interpreter
24. Train
25. Many

Sign Language Games

ABC Game

Starting with the first letter of the alphabet, each person will fingerspell an item in the selected category. Each person will repeat all previous fingerspelled words before adding their own selection. No duplicating is allowed. The categories can be of your choosing—for example: food, clothing, animals, occupations, furniture, drinks, plants, books, movies, music/musical instruments, etc. The last person can choose the next category. This game can also be played with signs instead of fingerspelling each word or both signs and fingerspelling can be combined during the game.

Color Game

Sign or fingerspell as many items as you can in thirty seconds that are the color red, blue, green, yellow, orange, white, pink, purple, brown, or black. This game requires a larger acquisition of signs.

Facial Expression and Body Language Game

A narrator reads a children's story, such as *Goldilocks*, *The Three Little Pigs*, *Snow White*, or *Cinderella*. Friends, family members, or students act out the parts using facial expression, body language, mime, and gestures. Only limited sign is needed for this game.

Knock Knock Game

There is a knock on the door. The player opens an imaginary door, and using facial expression, body language, mime, and gesture only, he or she will attempt to convey the message on the index card. Write any of the following, plus whatever else you may want to invent, on an index card for each player.

Knock Knock, open the imaginary door:

- You find a very large box wrapped up in beautiful paper, but it is too big to bring it through the door.
- You find a puppy.
- You find a man delivering a vase with roses.
- You find something very disgusting and slimy.
- You find a bag of rubbish.
- You find one million dollars.
- You find a very heavy box.
- You find a family of raccoons.
- You find another door.
- You find an old friend.
- You find a pizza delivery.
- You find a full-length mirror.
- You find a tornado.
- You find a photographer snapping your picture.
- You find a shiny new -

(Sign Language Games continued on next page) ▶

Sign Language Games (continued)

Brown Bag Game

Place three to five items in a small brown paper bag. Then describe each item using signs, fingerspelling if needed for brand names, acting out using the item if applicable, facial expression, body language, mime, and gestures. A more advanced level of this game can be played by placing three to five items in a brown bag that have related importance to the player. The player will describe each item and why the item is important to them. Examples:

- A bag of beach sand might be an important memory from a fabulous vacation getaway.
- A picture of a family member, a family animal, place, or thing.
- A souvenir from high school, college, and so forth.
- A letter, a book, or a movie ticket.
- Collectables, a piece of jewelry, and so forth.

Sign Opposites Game

One person signs a sentence or a single sign and the other person signs the opposite. Examples:

- up/down
- winter/summer
- start the car/stop the car
- open the door/close the door

Household Game

A person will act out the function of a household object. The receivers give the sign or writes out the name of the object. Examples:

- Unlocking a door: a key.
- Washing dishes: dish liquid or a dishwasher.
- Cleaning the floor: a broom, vacuum, or mop.

Twins Game

Choose a category such as trees, food, clothing, animals, or colors. Players are set up in pairs. A signal to start is given, and both players simultaneously fingerspell or sign only one item from the selected category. If the players fingerspell or sign the same item, they receive a point. The team with the most points wins.

Appendix B

Resources

Deaf/Sign Language Resources

ADCO Hearing Products, Inc.
5661 South Curtice Street
Littleton, CO 80120
Voice/TTY: (303) 794-3928 or (800) 726-0851
www.adcohearing.com

ALDA, Inc.
1131 Lake Street #204
Oak Park, IL 60301
Voice/Fax: (877) 907-1738
TTY: (708) 358-0135
www.alda.org

Americans with Disabilities Act
United States Department of Justice
Civil Rights Division
Voice: (800) 514-0301
TTY: (800) 514-0383
www.usdoj.gov/crt/ada

AT&T Relay Center
Relay Center Access: (800) 855-2881
Information: (800) 682-8786

Clarion by Advanced Bionics
Corporate Headquarters
Advanced Bionics Corporation
12740 San Fernando Road
Sylmar, CA 91342
Voice: (661) 362-1400 or (800) 678-2575
TTY: (800) 678-3575
www.cochlearimplant.com

CODA International, Inc.
P.O. Box 30715
Santa Barbara, CA 93130-0715
www.coda-international.org

Dawn Sign Press
6130 Nancy Ridge Drive
San Diego, CA 92121-3223
Voice/TTY: (858) 625-0600
www.dawnsign.com

Families for Hands and Voices
P.O. Box 371926
Denver, CO 80237
Phone: (303) 300-9763 or (866) 422-0422
www.handsandvoices.org

Gallaudet University
800 Florida Avenue NE
Washington, D.C. 20002
Voice/TTY: (202) 651-5000
www.gallaudet.edu

Garlic Press
1312 Jeppesen Ave.
Eugene, OR 97401
Phone: (541) 345-0063
www.garlicpress.com

Harris Communications
15155 Technology Drive
Eden Prairie, MN 55344-2277
Voice: (800) 825-6758
TTY: (800) 825-9187
www.harriscomm.com

National Association of the Deaf
814 Thayer Avenue
Silver Spring, MD 20910-4500
Voice: (301) 587-1788
TTY: (301) 587-1789
www.nad.org

National Association of the Deaf
1447 East Main Street
Spartanburg, SC 29307
Voice: (864) 585-1778 or (800) 237-6213
TTY: (864) 585-2617 or (800) 237-6819
Fax: (864) 585-2611 or (800) 538-5636
www.nad.org

National Education for Assistance Dogs Services (NEADS)
P.O. Box 213
West Boylston, MA 01583
www.neads.org

National Education for Assistance Dogs Services (NEADS) National Campus
305 Redemption Rock Trail South
Princeton, MA 01541
Voice/TDD: (978) 422-9064

National Technical Institute for the Deaf
Lyndon Baines Johnson Building
52 Lomb Memorial Drive
Rochester, NY 14623-5604
Voice/TTY: (716) 475-6700
www.rit.edu/NTID

National Theatre of the Deaf
55 Van Dyke Avenue, Suite 312
Hartford, CT 06106
Voice/TTY: (860) 724-5179 or (800) 300-5179
www.ntd.org

Registry of Interpreters for the Deaf, Inc.
333 Commerce Street
Alexandria, VA 22314
Voice: (703) 838-0030
TTY: (703) 838-0459
www.rid.org

Self-Help for Hard of Hearing People (SHHH)
7910 Woodmont Avenue, Suite 1200
Bethesda, MD 20814
Voice: (301) 657-2248
TTY: (301) 657-2249
www.shhh.org

Sign Media, Inc.
4020 Blackburn Lane
Burtonsville, MD 20866-1167
Phone: (800) 475-4756 or (301) 421-0268
www.signmedia.com

Soundbytes
108 Industrial Drive
Jersey City, NJ 07305
Voice/TTY: (888) 816-8191
www.soundbytes.com

Ultratec
450 Science Drive
Madison, WI 53711
Voice/TTY: (608) 238-5400
www.ultratec.com

Web Sites

American Society for Deaf Children:
   www.deafchildren.org
ASL Dictionary: *www.bconnex.net/~randys*
Deaf Education: *www.deafed.net*
DeafWeb Washington:
   www.deafweb.org/natlorgs.htm
Deaf Missions Official Online/Animated
   Dictionary of Religious Signs:
   www.deafmissions.com
Ear Surgery Information Center:
   www.earsurgery.org/cochlear.html
GG Wiz Mental Floss: *www.ggwiz/asl*
Handspeak: *www.handspeak.com*
KODA: *www.koda-info.org*
National Association of the Deaf Information
   Center: *www.nad.org/infocenter*
Say What Club: *www.saywhatclub.com*
Signing Online: *www.signingonline.com*

Sign Language Books

A Basic Course in American Sign Language,
   by Carol Padden, Tom Humphries, and
   Terrence O'Rourke.
American Sign Language, "The Green Books,"
   by Charlotte Baker-Shenk and Dennis
   Cokely.
*American Sign Language: A Comprehensive
   Dictionary,* by Martin L. A. Sternberg, Ed.D.
American Sign Language Medical Dictionary, by
   Elaine Costello.
American Sign Language Phrase Book,
   by Lou Fant.
American Sign Language the Easy Way, by
   David A. Stewart.
Conversational Sign Language II, by Willard
   Madsen.
Gallaudet Survival Guide to Signing, by
   Leonard G. Lane.

Handmade Alphabet, by Laura Rankin.

Learning American Sign Language, by Tom Humphries and Carol Padden.

Medical Sign Language, by W. Joseph Garcia and Charles C. Thomas.

Random House Webster's American Sign Language Dictionary, by Elaine Costello, Ph.D.

Religious Signing, by Elaine Costello.

Signing Made Easy, by Rod R. Butterwoth and Mickey Flodin.

Signs Across America, by Edgar H. Shroyer and Susan P. Shroyer.

Signs of the Times, by Edgar H. Shroyer.

The Joy of Signing, by Lottie L. Riekehof.

The Joy of Signing Puzzle Book, by Linda Lascelle Hillebrand.

The Joy of Signing Puzzle Book 2, by Linda Lascelle Hillebrand with Lottie L. Riekehof.

The Perigee Visual Dictionary of Signing, by Rod R. Butterworth.

Deaf Literature

A Deaf Adult Speaks Out, Third Edition, by Leo M. Jacobs.

A Loss for Words, by Lou Ann Walker.

A Man Without Words, by Susan Schaller.

American Deaf Culture: An Anthology, by Sherman Wilcox, ed.

Angels and Outcasts: An Anthology of Deaf Characters in Literature, by Trent Batson and Eugene Bergman, eds.

At Home Among Strangers, by Jerome D. Schein.

Deaf History Unveiled, by John V. VanCleve, ed.

Deaf in America: Voices from a Culture, by Carol Padden and Tom Humphries.

Deaf Like Me, by Thomas S. Spradley and James P. Spradley.

Deaf President Now!: The 1988 Revolution at Gallaudet University, by John B. Christiansen and Sharon N. Barnartt.

Everyone Here Spoke Sign Language: Hereditary Deafness on Martha's Vineyard, by Nora Ellen Groce.

I Have a Sister—My Sister Is Deaf, by Jeanne Whitehouse Peterson.

Mother Father Deaf: Living Between Sound and Silence, by Paul Michael Preston.

Seeing Voices, by Oliver Sacks.

The Mask of Benevolence: Disabling the Deaf Community, by Harlan Lane.

The Week the World Heard Gallaudet, by J. Gannon.

Train Go Sorry, by Leah Hager Cohen.

What's That Pig Outdoors?: A Memoir of Deafness, by Henry Kisor.

When the Mind Hears: A History of the Deaf, by Harlan Lane.

You and Your Deaf Child, by John W. Adams.

Video and CD-ROM

These titles are easily available online, through any of the resources we've listed here, or in any of your favorite local bookstores or retailers where videos and multimedia entertainment materials are sold.

The American Sign Language Dictionary
(CD-ROM)
American Sign Language Vocabulary (CD-ROM)
Baby See 'n Sign
Children of a Lesser God
Cochlear Implants: Covering the Basics
DEAFology 101: Deaf Culture As Seen Through the Eyes
of a Deaf Humorist
From Mime to Sign
Sign with Your Baby
Signing Naturally
Sound and Fury

Glossary

A

acronym:
A word formed from the first letters of several words.

active hand:
The dominant hand; that is, the hand that moves when forming a sign.

ADA:
Americans with Disabilities Act.

American Manual Alphabet:
Twenty-six handshapes that represent the letters of the alphabet.

American Sign Language:
A visual language that is the primary means of communication for the Deaf.

audiogram:
A graph on which a hearing test result is recorded.

B

body shift:
The movement of the signer's upper torso to represent two or more characters in a story or conversation.

The "Broken Ear":
The national symbol that represents deafness.

C

classifiers:
A set of handshapes that represent categories, shape, size, and movement of objects.

cochlear implant:
A device surgically implanted into the skull to stimulate the auditory fibers allowing certain amounts of hearing.

CODA:
Acronym meaning "Children of Deaf Adults."

compound sign:
Combining two or more signs.

Contact Sign:
A form of communication that uses sign language in English word order and combines both elements of ASL and English. Also referred to as Pidgin Sign English.

cued speech:
A set of eight handshapes used in four different locations around the face and mouth to help a lip reader distinguish between different sounds that look similar.

D

deaf:
The term used to describe when the sense of hearing is nonfunctional for the purpose of everyday communication.

Deaf community:
Deaf people who share common values, experiences, and a language.

decibel:
A decibel, or dB, is a unit of measurement for the loudness of sound.

dominant hand:
The strong, active hand that is used when signing.

F

fingerspelling:
The application of the manual alphabet to spell out words in full or abbreviated form.

G

GA:
The abbreviation for "go ahead" when typing on a TTY/TDD.

Gallaudet University:
The only liberal arts college exclusively for the Deaf in the United States.

gesture:
A body movement used in communicating.

grammar:
The principles, structure, and rules of a language.

H

handshape:
The shape of the hand, fingers, and palm when forming a sign.

I

iconic signs:
Signs that resemble objects.

initialized signs:
Signs that borrow letters from the manual alphabet.

interpreter:
A person who translates spoken language into sign language and/or sign language into spoken language.

K

KODA:
Acronym meaning "Kids of Deaf Adults."

L

lip reading:
The ability to observe lip movement in order to understand oral language.

M

modified signs:
Signs that have been changed, compressed, or altered.

N

neutral space:
The space in front of the signer's chest.

nonmanual:
Refers to behaviors that use head movement, facial expression, body language, and eye movement, and does not involve the hands.

O

OIC:
The abbreviation for "Oh, I see" when typing on a TTY/TDD.

oralism:
A method of communicating and educating a deaf person without the use of sign language.

P

postlingual deaf:
Term used to describe a person whose deafness occurs after language is acquired.

prelingual deaf:
Term used to describe a person whose deafness occurs at birth or before language is acquired.

PSE:
Pidgin Sign English, a form of communication that uses sign language in English word order and combines both elements of ASL and English. Also referred to as Contact Sign.

Q

Q:
The abbreviation that is used when asking a question during a TTY/TDD conversation.

R

relay service:
A service that provides a connection between a TTY user and a hearing person and uses a communication assistant, referred to as a CA.

S

sign language:
A manual language that uses symbols to represent ideas and concepts.

Signed English:
A signing system that is used to represent spoken English.

signer:
A person who uses sign language.

sim-com/simultaneous communication:
Manual and oral communication used simultaneously.

SK:
The abbreviation for "stop keying" when typing on a TTY/TDD.

speech reading:
The ability to observe lip movement in order to understand oral language.

synonym:
A word that is different from but expresses the same meaning as another word.

syntax:
The order in which words or signs are placed to form sentences and phrases.

T

timeline:
An imaginary line through the body extending in front and behind.

total communication:
The application of all methods of communicating.

TTY/TDD:
A telecommunication device for the deaf which acts as a telephone.

V

variation:
Differences in the formation and production of vocabulary.

Index

An *italicized* main heading indicates a discussion of the sign for that word.

THE EVERYTHING SERIES!

BUSINESS

Everything® Business Planning Book
Everything® Coaching and Mentoring Book
Everything® Fundraising Book
Everything® Home-Based Business Book
Everything® Landlording Book
Everything® Leadership Book
Everything® Managing People Book
Everything® Negotiating Book
Everything® Online Business Book
Everything® Project Management Book
Everything® Robert's Rules Book, $7.95
Everything® Selling Book
Everything® Start Your Own Business Book
Everything® Time Management Book

COMPUTERS

Everything® Computer Book

COOKBOOKS

Everything® Barbecue Cookbook
Everything® Bartender's Book, $9.95
Everything® Chinese Cookbook
Everything® Chocolate Cookbook
Everything® Cookbook
Everything® Dessert Cookbook
Everything® Diabetes Cookbook
Everything® Fondue Cookbook
Everything® Grilling Cookbook
Everything® Holiday Cookbook
Everything® Indian Cookbook
Everything® Low-Carb Cookbook
Everything® Low-Fat High-Flavor Cookbook
Everything® Low-Salt Cookbook
Everything® Mediterranean Cookbook
Everything® Mexican Cookbook
Everything® One-Pot Cookbook
Everything® Pasta Cookbook
Everything® Quick Meals Cookbook
Everything® Slow Cooker Cookbook
Everything® Soup Cookbook

Everything® Thai Cookbook
Everything® Vegetarian Cookbook
Everything® Wine Book

HEALTH

Everything® Alzheimer's Book
Everything® Anti-Aging Book
Everything® Diabetes Book
Everything® Dieting Book
Everything® Hypnosis Book
Everything® Low Cholesterol Book
Everything® Massage Book
Everything® Menopause Book
Everything® Nutrition Book
Everything® Reflexology Book
Everything® Reiki Book
Everything® Stress Management Book
Everything® Vitamins, Minerals, and
    Nutritional Supplements Book

HISTORY

Everything® American Government Book
Everything® American History Book
Everything® Civil War Book
Everything® Irish History & Heritage Book
Everything® Mafia Book
Everything® Middle East Book

HOBBIES & GAMES

Everything® Bridge Book
Everything® Candlemaking Book
Everything® Card Games Book
Everything® Cartooning Book
Everything® Casino Gambling Book, 2nd Ed.
Everything® Chess Basics Book
Everything® Crossword and Puzzle Book
Everything® Crossword Challenge Book
Everything® Drawing Book
Everything® Digital Photography Book
Everything® Easy Crosswords Book
Everything® Family Tree Book

Everything® Games Book
Everything® Knitting Book
Everything® Magic Book
Everything® Motorcycle Book
Everything® Online Genealogy Book
Everything® Photography Book
Everything® Poker Strategy Book
Everything® Pool & Billiards Book
Everything® Quilting Book
Everything® Scrapbooking Book
Everything® Sewing Book
Everything® Soapmaking Book

HOME IMPROVEMENT

Everything® Feng Shui Book
Everything® Feng Shui Decluttering Book, $9.95
Everything® Fix-It Book
Everything® Homebuilding Book
Everything® Home Decorating Book
Everything® Landscaping Book
Everything® Lawn Care Book
Everything® Organize Your Home Book

EVERYTHING® KIDS' BOOKS

All titles are $6.95

Everything® Kids' Baseball Book, 3rd Ed.
Everything® Kids' Bible Trivia Book
Everything® Kids' Bugs Book
Everything® Kids' Christmas Puzzle
    & Activity Book
Everything® Kids' Cookbook
Everything® Kids' Halloween Puzzle
    & Activity Book
Everything® Kids' Hidden Pictures Book
    Everything® Kids' Joke Book
Everything® Kids' Knock Knock Book
Everything® Kids' Math Puzzles Book
Everything® Kids' Mazes Book
Everything® Kids' Money Book

All Everything® books are priced at $12.95 or $14.95, unless otherwise stated. Prices subject to change without notice.

Everything® Kids' Monsters Book
Everything® Kids' Nature Book
Everything® Kids' Puzzle Book
Everything® Kids' Riddles & Brain Teasers Book
Everything® Kids' Science Experiments Book
Everything® Kids' Soccer Book
Everything® Kids' Travel Activity Book

KIDS' STORY BOOKS

Everything® Bedtime Story Book
Everything® Bible Stories Book
Everything® Fairy Tales Book

LANGUAGE

Everything® Conversational Japanese Book
    (with CD), $19.95
Everything® Inglés Book
Everything® French Phrase Book, $9.95
Everything® Learning French Book
Everything® Learning German Book
Everything® Learning Italian Book
Everything® Learning Latin Book
Everything® Learning Spanish Book
Everything® Sign Language Book
Everything® Spanish Phrase Book, $9.95
Everything® Spanish Verb Book, $9.95

MUSIC

Everything® Drums Book (with CD), $19.95
Everything® Guitar Book
Everything® Home Recording Book
Everything® Playing Piano and Keyboards Book
Everything® Rock & Blues Guitar Book
    (with CD), $19.95
Everything® Songwriting Book

NEW AGE

Everything® Astrology Book
Everything® Dreams Book
Everything® Ghost Book
Everything® Love Signs Book, $9.95
Everything® Meditation Book
Everything® Numerology Book
Everything® Paganism Book
Everything® Palmistry Book
Everything® Psychic Book
Everything® Spells & Charms Book
Everything® Tarot Book
Everything® Wicca and Witchcraft Book

PARENTING

Everything® Baby Names Book
Everything® Baby Shower Book
Everything® Baby's First Food Book
Everything® Baby's First Year Book
Everything® Birthing Book
Everything® Breastfeeding Book
Everything® Father-to-Be Book
Everything® Get Ready for Baby Book
Everything® Getting Pregnant Book
Everything® Homeschooling Book
Everything® Parent's Guide to Children
    with Asperger's Syndrome
Everything® Parent's Guide to Children
    with Autism
Everything® Parent's Guide to Children
    with Dyslexia
Everything® Parent's Guide to Positive Discipline
Everything® Parent's Guide to Raising a
    Successful Child
Everything® Parenting a Teenager Book
Everything® Potty Training Book, $9.95
Everything® Pregnancy Book, 2nd Ed.
Everything® Pregnancy Fitness Book
Everything® Pregnancy Nutrition Book
Everything® Pregnancy Organizer, $15.00
Everything® Toddler Book
Everything® Tween Book

PERSONAL FINANCE

Everything® Budgeting Book
Everything® Get Out of Debt Book
Everything® Homebuying Book, 2nd Ed.
Everything® Homeselling Book
Everything® Investing Book
Everything® Online Business Book
Everything® Personal Finance Book
Everything® Personal Finance in Your
    20s & 30s Book
Everything® Real Estate Investing Book
Everything® Wills & Estate Planning Book

PETS

Everything® Cat Book
Everything® Dog Book
Everything® Dog Training and Tricks Book
Everything® Golden Retriever Book
Everything® Horse Book
Everything® Labrador Retriever Book
Everything® Poodle Book

Everything® Puppy Book
Everything® Rottweiler Book
Everything® Tropical Fish Book

REFERENCE

Everything® Car Care Book
Everything® Classical Mythology Book
Everything® Einstein Book
Everything® Etiquette Book
Everything® Great Thinkers Book
Everything® Philosophy Book
Everything® Psychology Book
Everything® Shakespeare Book
Everything® Toasts Book

RELIGION

Everything® Angels Book
Everything® Bible Book
Everything® Buddhism Book
Everything® Catholicism Book
Everything® Christianity Book
Everything® Jewish History & Heritage Book
Everything® Judaism Book
Everything® Koran Book
Everything® Prayer Book
Everything® Saints Book
Everything® Understanding Islam Book
Everything® World's Religions Book
Everything® Zen Book

SCHOOL & CAREERS

Everything® After College Book
Everything® Alternative Careers Book
Everything® College Survival Book
Everything® Cover Letter Book
Everything® Get-a-Job Book
Everything® Job Interview Book
Everything® New Teacher Book
Everything® Online Job Search Book
Everything® Personal Finance Book
Everything® Practice Interview Book
Everything® Resume Book, 2nd Ed.
Everything® Study Book

SELF-HELP/ RELATIONSHIPS

Everything® Dating Book
Everything® Divorce Book
Everything® Great Sex Book

All Everything® books are priced at $12.95 or $14.95, unless otherwise stated. Prices subject to change without notice.

Everything® Kama Sutra Book
Everything® Self-Esteem Book

SPORTS & FITNESS

Everything® Body Shaping Book
Everything® Fishing Book
Everything® Fly-Fishing Book
Everything® Golf Book
Everything® Golf Instruction Book
Everything® Knots Book
Everything® Pilates Book
Everything® Running Book
Everything® T'ai Chi and QiGong Book
Everything® Total Fitness Book
Everything® Weight Training Book
Everything® Yoga Book

TRAVEL

Everything® Family Guide to Hawaii
Everything® Family Guide to New York City,
    2nd Ed.

Everything® Family Guide to Washington D.C.,
    2nd Ed.
Everything® Family Guide to the Walt Disney
    World Resort®, Universal Studios®,
    and Greater Orlando, 4th Ed.
Everything® Guide to Las Vegas
Everything® Guide to New England
Everything® Travel Guide to the Disneyland
    Resort®, California Adventure®,
    Universal Studios®, and the
    Anaheim Area

WEDDINGS

Everything® Bachelorette Party Book, $9.95
Everything® Bridesmaid Book, $9.95
Everything® Creative Wedding Ideas Book
Everything® Elopement Book, $9.95
Everything® Father of the Bride Book, $9.95
Everything® Groom Book, $9.95
Everything® Jewish Wedding Book
Everything® Mother of the Bride Book, $9.95
Everything® Wedding Book, 3rd Ed.

Everything® Wedding Checklist, $7.95
Everything® Wedding Etiquette Book, $7.95
Everything® Wedding Organizer, $15.00
Everything® Wedding Shower Book, $7.95
Everything® Wedding Vows Book, $7.95
Everything® Weddings on a Budget Book, $9.95

WRITING

Everything® Creative Writing Book
Everything® Get Published Book
Everything® Grammar and Style Book
Everything® Grant Writing Book
Everything® Guide to Writing a Novel
Everything® Guide to Writing Children's Books
Everything® Screenwriting Book
Everything® Writing Well Book